AN INTRODUCTION
CHRISTIAN SPIRITUALITY

AN INTRODUCTION
TO CHRISTIAN
SPIRITUALITY

—

Edited by
Ralph Waller and Benedicta Ward

SPCK

First published in Great Britain in 1999 by
Society for Promoting Christian Knowledge
Holy Trinity Church
Marylebone Road
London NW1 4DU

The publisher acknowledges with thanks permission
to reproduce an extract from the following:
'Little Gidding', in *Collected Poems 1909–1962* by T. S. Eliot,
Faber and Faber Ltd

British Library Cataloguing-in-Publication Data
A catalogue record for this book is available from the British Library

ISBN 0–281–05226–3

Typeset by Wilmaset Ltd, Birkenhead, Wirral
Printed in Great Britain by
The Cromwell Press, Trowbridge, Wiltshire

CONTENTS

Dedicated to
John Tudor
in friendship and gratitude

PREFACE

Interest in 'spirituality' continues to flourish, until the term seems to be synonymous with any way of making yourself feel better, whether it uses the tarot, the zodiac, the occult, magic, the paranormal, a back-to-nature syndrome, or simply techniques for relaxation. All these ways of 'spirituality' suggest systems able to make us better in tune with our universe and this is all very well until we find ourselves controlled by and limited by these external methods. And this suggests to Christians there must be more freedom and life to 'spirituality' than that, since 'spirituality' has always been a basic and dynamic part of the Christian life. There is a theological way of understanding the term, in which it stands for 'life in the Spirit' and which has a history as long as Christianity itself. The examination of the principles behind this tradition offers a new way forward in undertaking the search for a true, personal and dynamic 'spirituality' today. It was with this in mind that this book was compiled.

The papers assembled here originated in a series of lectures on Christian spirituality offered for three years in succession in connection with an examination paper on that topic in Oxford University Faculty of Theology, which was itself a response to the interest of students in this area. Four of the papers were meant as background to the specific texts the students would use, but, while these were four of the key areas for such study, it was found necessary to respond to a wider interest in the subject both by widening the four papers themselves and by offering discussion of another four major themes and areas.

The four specific areas were dealt with in Bishop Kallistos's examination of patristic spirituality, with special reference to the works of Evagrius and Gregory of Nyssa, expanding this to a discussion of the nature of the Christian response to the mystery of God by a denial of images. The second specific discussion was of two of the English mystics, Julian of Norwich and the author of the *Cloud of Unknowing*, which widened into an examination of the background of the English mystical tradition in the fourteenth century. Thirdly, the key area for the analysis of Christian spirituality is, of course, the works of the sixteenth-century Spanish mystics, and Dr Colin Thompson discussed the major contribution of both Teresa of Avila and John of the Cross. Fourthly, Ron Glithero then discussed the later use of the tradition of spirituality in the world of the Reformation.

Bishop Rowan's lecture was the first of the more general papers and dealt with the concept of spirituality and what it means for Christians in particular. The Reverend David Moss examined the theme of friendship in the early Church and the Middle Ages as a relevant concept in Christian understanding of spirituality today. Dr Ralph Waller gave a general paper on the basis of spirituality of the eighteenth and nineteenth centuries for the unity of Christians today, with special reference to James Martineau. Bishop Geoffrey concluded the course with an exposition of the distinctively Anglican approach to the theme with special reference to the seventeenth-century divines.

Thus these papers have emerged out of precise and scholarly examination of texts but they have all expanded from that basis. They have cohered into an overview of what spirituality means within the context of Christianity and are offered as an introduction to the ways in which Christians can talk about and undertake spirituality today, using the main lines of the past as a gift and guide to the future.

The editors would like to thank the Fellows and staff of Harris Manchester College for their hospitality to the lecturers, Judith Nisbet and Patricia Edwards for her help with typing the manuscript and Simon Kingston of SPCK for his patience and enthusiasm for this project.

Benedicta Ward
Ralph Waller

Contributors

Ronald Glithero: Formerly Head of Religious Studies, Westminster College, Oxford, Tutor to Farmington Fellows at Harris Manchester College, Oxford.

David Moss: Director of Studies at St Stephen's House, Oxford.

The Very Reverend Bishop, Dr Geoffrey Rowell: Bishop of Basingstoke. Formerly Chaplain and Fellow of Keble College, Oxford.

Dr Colin Thompson: Fellow of St Catherine's College, Oxford, and Lecturer in Spanish in the Faculty of Modern Languages.

Dr Ralph Waller: Principal of Harris Manchester College, Oxford.

Sister Benedicta Ward SLG: Reader in the History of Christian Spirituality in the University of Oxford and Honorary Lecturer at Harris Manchester College.

The Very Reverend Bishop, Dr Kallistos Ware: Orthodox Bishop of Dioklia. Spalding Lecturer in the University of Oxford and Fellow of Pembroke College, Oxford.

The Very Reverend Bishop, Dr Rowan Williams: Bishop of Monmouth. Previously Lady Margaret Professor of Divinity and Canon of Christ Church, Oxford.

TO STAND WHERE CHRIST STANDS

ROWAN WILLIAMS

It might be as well to begin with a few thoughts about what Christian spirituality is not. It is an area which is constantly in need of a certain level of 'demythologizing', given that the word 'spiritual' has lately become strangely fashionable. The cultivation of 'spirit', the promotion of 'spiritual values' in our educational system, the sense that there is in our human life a rather elusive but probably quite important area that needs attention and that can be described as the 'spiritual' – all this encourages the idea that spirituality is primarily a way of developing a dimension of your humanity, exercising a neglected limb or muscle. It will easily be associated with therapies of various kinds, tactics for living harmoniously with the world (and with your own responses to the world), and it will therefore tend to see the world as presenting a set of difficulties to be overcome by the practice of wisdom of one sort or another. In such terms, it commands a good deal of tolerance (a prime spiritual virtue, of course), even from those who would regard religious commitment of a traditional kind as suspect

There is nothing intrinsically wrong or stupid in this, and the notion that it might be a good idea to pay attention to how you live harmoniously in an environment that will pretty persistently hurt and frustrate you is a step forward. But if we want to understand the texts of the Christian spiritual tradition, we have to take several steps back from what might seem obvious these days about the nature of 'spirituality', since these contemporary categories will not take us very far; we shall frequently find ourselves baffled by the texts when they do not immediately or obviously reflect a wisdom about living in a complex environment. In contrast, they offer a radical redescription of that environment, in which the goals of human effort are not self-evident but need to be imagined and realized by a discipline wholly dependent on a number of fundamental beliefs about humanity and its maker. These are texts about how you come to be a native of a particular moral and imaginative world, so that you come to see and think yourself afresh. The task of learning techniques – not at all as alien to the Christian spiritual enterprise as some might imagine – is inseparable from the task of occupying a certain sort of place, grasping in a certain way where and who you are; and this place is specified not by any detached account of human beings in the universe but by a specific historical story and identity.

This becomes very clear if we look at what the very word 'spirit' means in the earliest Christian texts. Although St Paul can speak – so it seems – of a threefold structure to our human existence, body, soul and spirit (1 Thess. 5.23), it is fairly clear from the rest of his work that 'spirit' is very far from being simply an area of human experience or a portion of the human constitution. As the major epistles make plain, living in or according to 'spirit' (and it is seldom clear whether this means simply and directly the Spirit of God or whether it includes ourselves as 'spiritual') is a designation of the entire set of our human relations, to God and each other and our environment. We are delivered from life according to 'flesh' which is defined consistently as life dominated by self-directed instinct – so that we may live 'no longer for ourselves' (2 Cor. 5.15), but live in *koinonia*, that is, in the kind of relations to each other that are characterized by the passion for the other's good or welfare, and in the kind of relation to God that is characterized by the prayer Jesus himself prays, 'Abba, Father' (Rom. 8.5; Gal. 4.6). Thus is our 'place' defined: we stand where Jesus stands as Christian believers, and pray as Jesus prays; and in standing in that place before God as 'Abba', we share equally in Jesus' directedness towards the good and the healing of the world. Placed together in the place of Jesus, we are bound in *koinonia* towards each other, seeing one another not as rivals but as embodying a divine gift. Life in the spirit is life beyond the boundaries erected between ourselves and each other and ourselves and God (even, it is tempting to add, between ourselves and ourselves, since the divine Spirit, we are told, draws out of us what we did not know we desired (Rom. 8.26). Life in the spirit is life that is decisively free from the obsessions of self-justification, since the place of Jesus is the place of the one whom the Father has eternally said Yes to; there is no need to

2

negotiate for space or argue for favour and privilege, as it is always already given to and through Jesus.

It is in this very basic Christian theological perspective that we must look for the heart of Christian spirituality, since the life of the spirit cannot, in such a context, ever be an area of concern, merely a dimension of a wider life; it is the life of the believer, material and imaginative and desirous. Which is why the study of 'spirituality' constantly spills over into thinking about doctrine, ethics, art and all sorts of things besides. The Christian writer dealing with spirituality is writing essentially about what it is for a whole human life to be lived in the 'place' defined by Jesus. In the rest of this chapter, I want to look at some of the things that might be involved in occupying that place, particularly as they have been understood by some of the early and medieval writers in the tradition.

What makes the idea of the 'place' of Jesus Christ a complex thing to get hold of is that we have a narrative about Jesus at the heart of our faith as Christians; so that there are several moments and pictures that are associated with Jesus, and it is not possible to give a once-for-all static account of what is involved in the imitation of Christ. Jesus is a prophet and healer; Jesus prays with unique intimacy to God as Abba; Jesus is crucified and reviled; Jesus is raised to the heavenly places. And, for early Christian writers, there is a further dimension, in that Jesus is also the eternal Word of God made flesh; thus there is a kind of story to be told (an admittedly odd one) about the Word abandoning heavenly glory to become human; and a model of the eternal Word pouring himself out in adoration towards the Father and acting as the channel of the Father's creative love. How you talk about the life of the 'spirit' in such a connection will depend a lot on which story, which image, you settle on as central, or even (simply) which image works at this time for these purposes. If, then, we look, to begin with, at the theologies that dominated the schools of Alexandria in the second and third centuries, the theologies associated with Clement and Origen, we find at the centre of their account of the Christian life a set of ideas which most of us today would not instinctively associate with imitating Jesus, since we tend to focus upon the historical prophet and healer where they consistently turned towards the eternal life of the

Word, the Logos. Jesus embodies a heavenly reality that is not quite on the same level as the ultimate source of everything, the one true God, yet is the way the one true God exercises his life. The Logos is, we could say, the shape of God's action, the channel through which the divine life flows as it acts. The divine life expresses itself as balance and harmony: the ultimate source is pure unity, but, as this source acts and moves, it does so in a way that makes possible the coexistence of different realities in a harmonious, not a chaotic relationship. For Origen in particular, this expression of the divine will and action was eternal, always flowing out from God; and also it was itself a centre of action, in the sense that it was turned towards God in contemplation: the outflowing of divine action was balanced by the answering rhythm of contemplative love returning to the one source. The true destiny of the creation is to be united with that answering rhythm: the life of the spirit is to be one with the Logos.

The human Jesus is the one created being that is in perfect alignment with the life of the Logos; he lives a perfectly 'reasonable' life. Such terminology is, of course, very strange to our ears, since we tend to think of reasonableness as if it meant simply being judicious or unemotional or prudent. It is a rather negative and very prosaic word. But for a writer like Origen and many of those who followed him, the reasonable life was one of absorbed bliss, contemplation of the beauty and simplicity of the divine life, freedom from the distractions of specific impressions drawn from the material world around and freedom from 'passion', from the realm of reactive and self-oriented instinct and feeling. Limited, earthly images and aspirations drop away; the spirit returns to what it was made for, a life that simply reflects back to God with love God's own supremely active and unified nature in a harmony of love. The unbroken union of the Logos with Jesus makes it possible for us to have released in us the freedom to be our proper spiritual selves. But one implication of this, an implication that many generations of Christians have found problematic, was that the concrete reality of Jesus' earthly life was of less spiritual interest in itself than the eternal life of the Logos which it embodied: the goal was not so much to imitate Jesus of Nazareth as to be at one with the heavenly Word. The narrative

4

of Jesus was always pointing beyond itself, and to remain focused upon this would be to remain in a kind of slavery to the impressions of the world of the senses.

Here, then, the place of Jesus is finally the place of the Logos before the mystery of the Father, a mystery never fully penetrated or sounded. To arrive at this place requires an inner resolution of the tensions between the contemplative spirit and the pressures of emotion and instinct ('passion'), so that the spirit becomes free for the vision of God; and the goal of harmony with the Logos suggests also that our ultimate freedom is also an other-related balance with the rest of the created order – at least, the created order in its own inner truth and balance. The tradition stemming from Origen in particular emphasized the importance of aligning your mind with the reasonable, ordered structure of a universe created by a rational, self-consistent God. Similarly, the journey to spiritual freedom must involve an alignment with the inner harmony of the Bible, which, like the universe as a whole, is the expression of a unified and rational wisdom under the guise of an apparently diverse and even conflict-ridden surface. The spiritual reader of the Bible discerns what is beneath the surface, the spiritual sense of the biblical narratives and injunctions, and learns to sit a bit light to the apparent (but potentially deceptive) surface difficulties.

The risks in this vision were clear to a good many early Christian thinkers; did all this not suggest too radical a schism between the spirit and its earthly casing? Did the spiritual reading of Scripture not risk making the real meaning of the Bible something quite divorced from the historical narratives? Did the emphasis on the heavenly Logos not draw our attention dangerously far from the fleshly Jesus who speaks to us as we are, beings of flesh and blood? There were those who, while deeply sympathetic to Origen and marked by his influence, struggled to avoid some of these dangers, in various ways. One of the most significant of these was the great fourth-century theologian, Gregory of Nyssa, the most original and profound of that extraordinary group of thinkers, the Cappadocian Fathers, who, in the second half of the fourth century, established the classical vocabulary for thinking about God as Trinity. Gregory is careful to qualify anything that might lead us to think that the spirit is simply stronger and better than the body. The body itself is a kind of reflection of the spirit, on the one hand, and the spirit itself, because it is created, is always falling short of the full reality of God. But there is a further important point: God is clearly understood by Gregory and his circle as eternally and necessarily Father, Son and Holy Spirit, not as a primordial transcendent Father whose mysteries are mediated to the lower regions by the Logos as a deputy. The Son and Spirit share fully the divine life. Thus it will not quite do simply to underline the goal of spiritual life as alignment with the Logos. Gregory can, in a way rather reminiscent of Origen, talk of how we take our stand on the 'rock' of Jesus Christ so as to see the divine mystery, but at the same time we are placed upon the rock so that we can see God 'passing by'. Gregory is here interpreting the strange story about Moses in Exodus 33, where Moses asks to see God's glory, and God replies by promising to show Moses only his back as he passes by, since no one can see God's face and live. Gregory goes on to allude to the instruction of Christ in the Gospels that we are to follow him: you do not see the face of someone you are following. In other words, our vision of the glory of God is inseparable from the following of Jesus Christ; if we ask how Gregory understands being in the 'place' of Jesus, the answer is, paradoxically, that it is to be always moving in the direction of Jesus' movement, and moving not simply in our strength but being carried along by him.

This points up two very fundamental insights in Gregory's writing. He explores the Christian life in his greatest work on the subject, *The Life of Moses*, by reflection on the Exodus stories. We are delivered from slavery, slavery to selfishness and envy and so on, and then led into the desert; the journey reaches its climax at Mount Sinai, where Moses climbs up into the dense cloud at the mountain's peak, to meet God in darkness. So the life of the spirit is a life always in motion, never arriving at a final and satisfying level of comprehension; and it is a life that leads us into 'unknowing': the spirit, a created and limited reality, can never compass the whole of God's life, and the best we can hope for is to be swept up into the Son's journey towards the Father, his eternal and temporal pouring of his life into the life of the Father who eternally pours his life into the Son. The emphasis here is subtly but distinctly different from what we find in Origen; Origen's picture sees the goal of Christian life as a vision cleared of all compromising elements of the diverse and distracting world; Gregory seems to envisage a goal that is both seeing and not-seeing, a vision that is never free of some element we might call 'desire' – though he is agonizedly careful, in other works, in trying to find a way of saying this that will not suggest that we are eternally dissatisfied or eternally yearning for something we lack that will give us gratification. The goal is, in a strange way, not being in the place of Jesus, but being never quite in the place of Jesus, always being taken along the road that his life in eternity and in history defines. And this is why elsewhere Gregory is clear that the following of Jesus entails a perfectly practical kind of service to and acceptance of one another, and why in *The Life of Moses* he has so much to say about the destructive evil of envy in the Christian life – looking at one another rather than the Christ who goes ahead.

In stressing the element of darkness and unfinishedness in the Christian journey, Gregory is not, of course, inventing a new theme, though he is undoubtedly giving it a quite new degree of sophisticated exposition. Following Jesus, and finding his 'place' through darkness, might well be a summary of what earlier Christian generations thought about martyrdom; and for the first three centuries of the Church's life the most obvious and compelling model for sharing the place of Christ was that of martyrdom. The martyr's body is, in a very strong sense, the place where Christ is: the second-century slave girl Felicitas anticipating her death in the arena said that 'another will be in me who will suffer for me, as I shall suffer for him'; and it was another slave girl, Blandina, whose body crucified before the pagan mob is described as an image of her Lord. The martyr is the 'site' of holiness not because she or he is showing exemplary courage or whatever, but because Christ is substantially present in that suffering body, as surely as Christ is present in the bread and wine of the Eucharist. Indeed, it is just this parallel that is evoked by two famous texts about martyrdom. Ignatius, Bishop of Antioch at the beginning of the second century, imagines his body being ground by the teeth of the animals in the arena so as to become bread for

God's people. A few decades later, Ignatius' friend, Polycarp, Bishop of Smyrna, is brought into the arena for execution; before the fire is lit he prays, in words that are clearly meant to remind us of the eucharistic prayer he would have offered each Sunday. His body is the eucharistic offering where Christ will become present; and we should not be surprised when, from the midst of the flames, there comes a smell like that of bread baking.

But the literature about martyrs focuses one of the major problems in the life of the early Church. Where Christ is must be where authority is to be found; Ignatius makes it abundantly clear that his forthcoming sufferings for the sake of Christ give his decisions and commendations a special force, even in advance of the event. Later on, Christians who had been imprisoned and tortured for their faith could claim various kinds of authority on their release, authority that sometimes seemed to clash with that of the local hierarchy. And when the authority of the person who had suffered for their faith was increasingly replaced (after the days of persecution were over) by the authority of the holy ascetic, the person who had voluntarily undertaken suffering for the sake of Christ, some of the same tensions reappeared. This is not simply a problem of church politics (though it is at least that, of course); in the light of what I have been arguing so far, it should be seen as a problem about where the place of Christ is to be identified most clearly. As recent research has emphasized, the tension was between recognizing Christ in the extraordinary achievement of the individual holy person and recognizing him in the corporate life, a life lived under visible systems of authority, of the Church. The sense in Ignatius or Polycarp of the extraordinary achievement of a martyr's death being a kind of sacramental offering to and for the entire Church shifted increasingly towards a more individualistic concentration on the charisma of the holy man or woman.

Both sides of this argument, which broke out very bitterly in Carthage in the mid-third century, Alexandria in the early fourth century and Asia Minor in the mid-fourth century, to give only the most dramatic examples, had some theological rationale to appeal to. The place of Christ is nothing if not a personal site, something concrete in a particular biography

8

and the particular location of a human body; yet the New Testament also makes it plain that the place of Christ is pre-eminently the common life, the *koinonia* of believers animated by the Holy Spirit. The difficult balance of these two factors left an abiding legacy to the Christian mind: the history of Christian 'spirituality' is full of instances of such a tension, of the double suspicion of individual charismatic authority and of unequivocal loyalty to historic authority. Christianity, of all the major world religious traditions, has had perhaps the most consistently restless attitude toward authority – which tells us something about the deeply suspicious culture of Western modernity that springs from Christian questionings (for good and ill). As a good many recent scholars have insisted, under-standing the Christian spiritual tradition can illuminate in remarkable ways our sense of our general cultural history. What Christians thought about their human integrity, the images they shaped of the self and its context, naturally moulded what could be thought about self and society as a whole – precisely because (to pick up an earlier point) they did not regard the spiritual as a privileged private area of feeling and self-cultivation.

One of the ways in which the Christian tradition shaped the sense of self for the cultures of the Mediterranean and Northern Europe (and so also for North America) relates to another central theme in the quest for the peace of Christ. The self is deeply and indeed fundamentally 'erotic' – that is, a subject of desire. We have already seen how Gregory of Nyssa struggles with the problem of how to inscribe something like desire in the heart of his account of the self growing eternally Godwards. Augustine, in the next generation after Gregory, writing in a very different language (literally: in Latin, not Greek), pursued the same theme with unparalleled imagina-tion and depth. In what sense, though, is this to do with the place of Christ? It may seem, as we saw with Gregory, to be a bafflingly paradoxical identification of Christ's place with the place of his absence, the place where he has always been before but is no longer. Something of the explanation of this is developed by using not merely an erotic but a nuptial idiom to speak of our place in relation to Christ's. We are where he is not; but that place where he is not is also the place where he is bound

9

to be as the lover or spouse of the created self. To be in the place of Christ is to be Christ's 'other' in a relation as intimate as that of sexual union within the covenant of marriage; the object of an eternal and unfailing commitment, the object – in the bold language that Christian theologians did not shrink from using, despite its philosophical problems – of divine 'desire'. The notion that Christ is the bridegroom of the Christian community is, of course, already there in the New Testament, where the ancient imagery of God as the husband of the people of Israel was taken up and transferred to God in Christ and the Israel of the Church; Ephesians and Revelation both witness eloquently to this usage. Origen seems to have been the first to offer a systematic interpretation of the Song of Songs in terms of Christ's love for the individual spirit and for the Church; and Gregory of Nyssa develops this a good deal further. In the Middle Ages, Bernard of Clairvaux's sermons on the Song furnish a classical example of how this exegesis blossomed, sometimes with what is to modern eyes a startling explicitness of erotic imagery. But its most sophisticated development is probably in St John of the Cross in the sixteenth century. John's poetry in particular plays with the figures of erotic absence and erotic enjoyment in order to bring into focus the paradoxes of being where Jesus is and where Jesus is not. 'The beloved' has been present – not only in the world at large (as the one who creates and orders it) but also as lover, as one who has been enjoyed. The created self is 'wounded' as a result of this encounter: virginity is lost, the self-containment of the fallen creature is breached, joy is offered and briefly tasted, and then there is withdrawal and absence. Yet (as John's theological commentaries on the poetry amplify) the spirit's experience in absence, in the darkness of not knowing who or what it is when deprived of the erotic affirmation given by the Saviour, confirms the spirit more deeply in the place of a Christ whose work reaches its climax in the experience of absence, of desire confronted with inescapable death. Christ's reduction to nothing in the inner and outer agony of the cross is what makes sense of the experience of the spirit in the anguish of dereliction; in that absence, the spirit is transformed to be more abidingly like Christ, its desire becoming more and more nothing but the utterly expectant, utterly hospitable openness of love such as exists eternally between the Father and the Word in the Spirit. The imagery of John's *Living Flame of Love* presupposes that the Holy Spirit as the agency of God transfiguring the spirit into divinity consumes the desire for specific worldly spiritual gratifications in order to make the spirit burn with the selfless desire of God for God (a paradoxical enough formulation, I know, but the only one that can quite express the radicality of what John is evoking).

Like his friend and directee Teresa, John believes that the place of Christ is the place of incarnation – that is, of God's dispossession of divine security or distance in order to be entirely present in the world of flesh and blood as a fleshly agent, suffering and dying as we do. Much of Teresa's discussion of her 'mystical' experience comes down, finally, to the affirmation of a new rooting in the reality of the present human moment before God; the huge disruptions of her emotional turmoil, her visions and communications, serve ultimately to return her as a displaced, dispossessed person to the present: to being a place where the hospitable openness of God's love as realized definitively in the incarnation of God the Son is humanly specific. John and Teresa experience and construct the process of dispossession in distinct ways, John always being more wary of the dramatic and tangible intrusions of grace in the physical experience of the believer, Teresa retaining a fascination (even if, in the long run, a chastened fascination) with the extraordinary and preternatural. But they agree in looking finally to Christ as the defining shape of their own journeys: for John, it is the passage to and through the 'night of the spirit', the final stripping away of all the systems and external reference points by which we seek to define ourselves, that brings us to where Christ is, as the intimate and inseparable other who can share his own intimate and inseparable otherness-in-love to the Father; for Teresa, it is the dizzying upheavals of God's insistent love, sensed in body and spirit, that shake out our own convincedness that we are in charge and lead us to be identified with the movement of the Word from the Father into the heart of the world (where in fact the Father already is, waiting expectantly for the Son to return to him). Between them, the Spanish Carmelites give an unprecedently consistent reading of the life of the spirit in terms of conformation to Christ incarnate. It is a pity that they have come to be seen as of interest to students of the 'abnormal' in religious experience – Teresa in particular – as if they were primarily interested in odd things happening to a privileged minority. Their own sense of what they were was clearly much more that they were seeking to grasp what was involved in being a baptized Christian in a serious way. They are, of course, as people of an age that was getting more and more interested in biography, in individual records of change and growth, far more closely focused upon the specifics of the self than most of their precursors (Teresa especially); but it is important not to think that their agenda was different in kind from that of their medieval and patristic ancestors.

A brief introductory note such as this cannot pretend to cover the whole range of the literature of classical Christian spirituality. What I hope it may do is to offer an interpretative pattern for reading other texts, a set of questions that might be worth asking. As I said at the beginning of this essay, if we approach Christian texts from any period before the nineteenth century with the primary question in our minds, 'What subjective experience are they trying to convey?' we shall be disappointed. We are so often encouraged to look for records of 'mystical experience' that we may miss what is most distinctive in what we read; we shall focus on phrases that suggest the sort of experience we think religious people ought to be having (encounters with the Transcendent, feelings of absorption or whatever), and we shall overlook the ways in which a text works to provide a broad imaginative territory in which the particular reader is letting himself or herself be defined afresh – how they are letting themselves be converted, if you like. This means that a good reading of a classical text in this area will always be one that attends to the entire rhythm of its argument and the detail of its imagery. The question is, 'What does this writer want me to see? What of my own story: am I being invited to retell or recast it in the light of the way the text presents the story of God's action in Jesus Christ? As has been indicated, some of these ways will be very odd to us; most of us will not start with much sense of what meditation on the eternal Logos might have meant for an Alexandrian ascetic in the third Christian century. We may find Gregory of Nyssa

on the imitation of the human compassion or even the divine
kenosis of Christ more approachable, closer to a twentieth-
century understanding of Christlikeness. But the underlying
issue is the same; given belief in a Saviour who is both human
and eternally active towards and on behalf of the divine
source of all, no one category is going to exhaust what might
be said about what it is to be where he is. Even without the
complex development that increasingly understood being with
Christ as being with him in his absence or otherness, it could
never have been possible to define Christ's place in terms of
one graspable image or ideal. Christian writers are constantly
having the wrong categories reconstructed by the alarming
plurality of images of Christ generated by their theological
and narrative heritage. And so far from this suggesting to
them any kind of radical pluralism or relativism in their theolo-
gizing, they concluded that they needed a theological framework spacious enough to allow for such a bewildering
multiplicity; a framework as broad as the whole discourse of
God and of humanity. The point has been made often enough,
but it is worth reiterating: the strains of classical theological
language are in substantial part due to the scope of these rede-
finitions of God and the human that insistently edged into
Christian speech through the corporate experiences of worship
and mission.

2

PRAYER IN EVAGRIUS OF PONTUS AND
THE MACARIAN HOMILIES

KALLISTOS WARE

The two currents

What is prayer? What aspect or faculty of our human person-hood do we chiefly employ when we call upon God? What part is played by the body during our prayer, and what part by the imagination?

Let us consider the answers to these questions provided by two dominant figures in the history of Christian spirituality, both dating from the late fourth century and both writing in Greek: Evagrius of Pontus, and the unknown author of the Macarian *Homilies*. Evagrius (*c.* 346–99) was an admirer of Origen, a disciple of St Gregory of Nazianzus, and during the last seventeen years of his life a monk in the Nitrian desert, not far from Alexandria in Egypt. The *Homilies*, on the other hand, are more difficult to date and place. They are ascribed to a Coptic ascetic living in the desert of Scetis (not far from Nitria), St Macarius of Egypt (*c.* 300–390), whom Evagrius knew personally; but it is generally agreed that this attribution is impossible. The background of the *Homilies* is in fact not Coptic but Syrian, and they seem to be connected with the Syrian ascetic movement known as Messalianism, even though not all the characteristic Messalian teachings appear in them. Probably they were written around 380–90 either in Syria itself or in Asia Minor. For convenience I shall call the author of the *Homilies* by the name 'Macarius', but his actual identity remains a mystery to us.[1]

At first sight, Evagrius and Macarius seem to exemplify two very different approaches to the spiritual life, although when they are examined more closely it becomes evident that the contrast between them is much less sharp than initially appears. Evagrius – to use the terminology of the great Jesuit specialist on Eastern Spirituality, Irénée Hausherr – expresses the standpoint of 'mystical intellectualism', while Macarius represents the tradition of 'mystical materialism' or 'the school of sentiment or of supernatural consciousness'.[2] While Evagrius is systematic, Macarius is unmethodical. Evagrius' approach is Platonist and philosophical, while that of Macarius is more biblical, more christocentric, more attentive to the role of the Holy Spirit. Evagrius emphasizes the intellect (*nous*), Macarius the heart (*kardia*), but these two terms, as we shall soon discover, need to be carefully defined. Evagrius regularly employs the word 'knowledge' (*gnosis*), while Macarius prefers to speak in terms of 'feeling' or 'perception' (*aisthesis*) and of 'assurance' (*plerophoria*).[3] Whereas the body is largely ignored in Evagrius, the Macarian *Homilies* have much to say about our physical transfiguration. In his understanding of prayer, Evagrius is deeply influenced by apophatic or negative theology; the higher levels of prayer, so he insists, should be non-iconic, free from all images and conceptual thinking. Macarius on the other hand is more cataphatic or affirmative in his approach (although he too has an apophatic side); he makes an abundant use of pictorial metaphors, and nowhere suggests that prayer should involve the shedding of all thoughts and images.

These contrasts, however, although useful as a starting-point, should not be pressed too far. There are similarities as well as differences between the two authors. For example, when speaking about union with God they both of them use the symbolism of light rather than darkness; they are both alike 'solar' rather than 'nocturnal' mystics.

'The communion of the intellect'

How, then, does Evagrius of Pontus understand the essence of prayer? At the outset of his classic work *On Prayer: One Hundred and Fifty-Three Texts*, he supplies a concise definition: 'Prayer is the communion of the intellect (*nous*) with God.'[4] Prayer, then, is an act of 'communion', a 'conversation' with God; and the faculty within us that enters into this communion is the *nous*. Evagrius reverts regularly to this basic understanding of what it means to pray. 'Undistracted prayer is the highest intellection (*noesis*) of the intellect (*nous*),' he writes. 'Prayer is the ascent of the intellect to God.'[5]

At once this raises the question what Evagrius means by the term *nous*. This is an altogether crucial point for any right understanding of Evagrian spirituality. Some translators render *nous* as 'mind'; but that is far too vague a word, for 'mind' can signify anything that goes on within our inner world – consciousness, thought, reasoning, remembrance, volition, feeling – whereas Evagrius has in view something much more specific. For want of a better equivalent, I shall use the English word 'intellect'; but that also can be misleading, for 'intellect' is commonly understood to denote ratiocination and discursive argumentation, and that is not at all what Evagrius has in view when he speaks of the *nous*.

To appreciate the Evagrian understanding of the *nous*, it is necessary to look back to Plato's *Republic*. In Book VI he makes a fourfold distinction between conjecture (*eikasia*), belief (*pistis*), thinking (*dianoia*), and intellection (*noesis*). The first two apply to the world of the senses, the world of shifting and inconstant appearances, while the last two apply to the realm of the intelligible Ideas or Forms, where alone certainty and enduring truth are to be found. Although the second pair, *dianoia* and *noesis*, both deal with the level of the intelligibles, there is an important difference between them. *Dianoia* denotes the apprehension of truth through the use of discursive thinking, that is to say, through reasoning from premises to a conclusion, as in mathematics. *Noesis*, on the other hand, signifies a higher faculty within the human person, whereby we apprehend the truth not through syllogistic argumentation but by a direct act of inner vision, a sudden flash of intuitive insight.[6]

Developing Plato's distinction, we may say that through *dianoia* we know *about* God, but through *nous* we know God. *Dianoia* works by means of dissection and analysis, and at this level the thinker is conscious of the object of his thought as being other than himself. But on the level of *noesis*, we no longer analyse and argue, but the truth is simply 'seen' to be true; the subject–object distinction disappears, and in an experience of undivided wholeness the *nous* is totally identified with that which (or the One whom) it contemplates – in T. S. Eliot's phrase, 'You are the music while the music lasts'. St

Maximus the Confessor (d. 662) describes this kind of 'intellection' (*noesis*) as 'simple and unified knowledge',[7] while his contemporary St Isaac of Nineveh (alias Isaac the Syrian) calls it 'simple cognition'. 'Accurate designations', writes the latter, 'can only be established concerning earthly things. The things of the Age to Come do not possess a true name, but [can be apprehended] only by simple cognition, which is exalted above all names and signs and forms and colours and habits and composite denominations.'[8] In this way, what Plato and the Fathers mean by *noesis* corresponds, not to what we today envisage by 'intellectual discussion', but – in part, at any rate – to what we would designate as 'mystical experience'. *Noesis* is not the kind of thing that we would expect to discover in the pages of an academic journal issued by a learned society; there for the most part we find only the fruits of the *dianoia*.

Now it is evident that when Evagrius employs the terms *nous* and *noesis*, he has precisely in view the kind of apprehension by 'simple cognition' to which Isaac refers. For, having defined prayer as 'the communion of the intellect with God', Evagrius at once goes on to ask: 'What state, then, does the intellect need so that it can reach out to its Lord without deflection and commune with Him *without any intermediary*?'[9] The *nous*, that is to say, when it attains the higher levels of prayer, 'communes' with God not through the medium of images, words and concepts, but in a non-discursive manner, through a direct experience of unmediated unity.

The intuitive, non-discursive sense that Evagrius gives to the term *nous* becomes clearer as the treatise *On Prayer* continues. 'When you are praying', he insists, 'do not shape within yourself any image of the Deity, and do not let your intellect be stamped with the impress of any form; but approach the Immaterial in a non-material manner, and then you will understand.'[10] He goes on to assert, in a famous epigram, 'Prayer is the shedding of thoughts'[11] – a 'putting away' or 'laying aside' of all images, ideas and concepts. Our abstract concepts, as St Gregory of Nyssa (d. *c.* 394) observes, are in danger of becoming a barrier between us and the direct apprehension of the living God; and so, giving to the Ten Commandments a figurative intepretation, Gregory commands us to smash the mental idols of God that we fashion within us.[12] In similar terms Evagrius teaches that the intellect in prayer is to be stripped 'naked'.[13] Our aim, he states, is 'pure prayer'[14] – prayer, that is to say, which is pure not merely from sinful thoughts but from *all* thoughts.

When Evagrius writes, 'Prayer is the shedding of thoughts', he does not of course intend this as a definition of all forms of praying. On the contrary, he allows an important place to what he calls 'psalmody' (*psalmodia*), namely the recitation of the Psalter – to what we today would call the Divine Office, although in Evagrius' day this was much simpler than in later monasticism. Clearly, such 'psalmody' involves the use of words, images and mental concepts. By the same token, Evagrius takes it for granted that the Christians for whom he is writing are taking a regular part in the Church's sacramental worship, even though in the work *On Prayer* he says little or nothing about this. The aphorism 'Prayer is the shedding of thoughts' refers only to one particular type of prayer: to the prayer of silence, of deep stillness, of listening to God and contemplative waiting upon him in single-hearted adoration.

Such is Evagrius' ideal: an inner state of contemplative 'gazing', free from all images and all discursive thinking. Not surprisingly, this makes him deeply reserved towards visionary experiences of any kind. God, he states, is 'beyond all sense-perception and all conceptual thinking (*ennoia*)' and 'does not possess quantity or form'.[15] Accordingly he urges: 'Never try to see a form or shape during the time of prayer. Do not try to see angels or Christ in a visible way . . . I shall say again what I have said elsewhere: blessed is the *nous* which at the time of prayer has gained complete freedom from forms (*amorphia*).'[16] 'The intellect', he writes, 'attains its full strength when it imagines nothing of the things of this world at the time of prayer.'[17] At this higher level of prayer, then, Evagrius allows no place for the *phantasia*, the image-making faculty or imagination. What he envisages is something altogether different from the discursive meditation recommended by Ignatius Loyola, François de Sales or Alphonsus Liguori.

Indeed, in its contemplation of God, the *nous* not only ceases to be aware of sensory images derived from the outside world, but it is no longer conscious of itself; the subject–object distinction disappears.[18] When we contemplate, he says, we no more know that we are contemplating than we are conscious of our own sleeping.[19] Evagrius goes so far as to affirm, 'Blessed is the *nous* which at the time of prayer has gained complete *anaisthesia*.'[20] The word *anaisthesia* could be translated 'freedom from sense-perception' or 'from sensation', but probably the true meaning is 'complete absence of self-awareness'. In the words of Evagrius' disciple, St John Cassian (d. after 430), 'A monk's prayer is not perfect if in the course of it he is aware of himself or of the fact that he is praying'.[21]

This loss of self-awareness surely comes close to what we today mean by mystical ecstasy. It is true that, when Evagrius employs the word *ekstasis*, he uses it – as Origen does[22] – in a derogatory sense, as signifying 'alienation' of the mind, 'derangement' or 'madness'.[23] Whereas St Gregory of Nyssa and the Areopagitic writings (*c.* 500) see prayer as a passing beyond the *nous* in ecstatic self-transcendence, according to Evagrius our aim in prayer is to achieve a vision of the 'proper state' (*katastasis*) of the intellect;[24] he is in this sense not 'ecstatic' but 'katastatic'. Yet, if we look beyond words to content, it becomes clear that in Evagrius' teaching 'pure prayer of the intellect', involving as it does a suspension of our conceptual thinking and our normal self-awareness, has certainly (in the modern sense of the word) an 'ecstatic' dimension. Thus, if Evagrius is styled an 'intellectual', it must at once be added that he is very far from being such in the usual contemporary meaning of this term.

If 'pure prayer' is specifically an activity of the *nous*, does the body have any positive part to play as we advance to the higher levels of contemplation? The answer seems to be that it does not. It is true that Evagrius does not regard the body as evil but affirms, on the contrary, that 'the body is often called the friend of the soul'.[25] But, faithful to the teaching of his master Origen, he regards the body as extrinsic to true personhood; our ultimate objective is to return to our original state, when each of us was a 'naked' intellect. Admittedly, he speaks in positive terms about the gift of tears, which is of course a bodily experience.[26] But, once a person has reached the level of 'pure prayer', there seems little or nothing that the body can contribute. 'Approach the Immaterial in a non-material manner', he says;[27] the final aim of the spiritual ascent seems to be to disincarnate ourselves and to return so far as possible, even in this present life, to our primal state as pure *nous*, unencumbered by the external clothing of our bodies.

If the body has no place in the more exalted stages of the mystical ascent, and if it is our objective to attain 'complete freedom from forms' (*amorphia*) and 'complete absence of self-awareness' (*anaisthesia*), then (it may be asked) is not the end of our journey a state of blank emptiness, not a plenitude of personal communion but an impersonal void? This is certainly a misinterpretation of Evagrius. The spiritual journey, in his view, leads not to vacuity but to an experience of non-material light. Initially this takes the form of a vision of the light of the intellect: 'It is a sign of dispassion (*apatheia*), when the *nous* begins to see its own light. . . .[28] In the time of prayer they see the light characteristic of intellect shining around them. . . .[29] If someone wishes to see the state of the intellect, let him deprive himself of all visual images; then he will see himself as sapphire and the colour of the sky.'[30] At this stage Evagrius is evidently referring to an experience of the created light inherent in the intellect; there are parallels here in Yoga.[31] But then he alludes to a higher experience in which the intellect beholds, not its own created light, but the uncreated and divine light: 'it will be totally mingled with the light of the Holy Trinity'.[32] Here he anticipates the teaching of St Gregory Palamas and the fourteenth-century Hesychasts, who speak about a vision of the uncreated light of Tabor. It should be emphasized that when Evagrius refers to a vision of light, whether created or uncreated, he envisages an experience of pure luminosity; no shape, form or face is actually seen in the light.[33]

The heart's perception

Turning from Evagrius of Pontus to the *Homilies* ascribed to Macarius, we are at once conscious of moving into a different world. Whereas Evagrius speaks of prayer as the communion of the intellect with God, Macarius sees it rather as the perception (*aisthesis*) of the heart. The term 'heart' (*kardia*) is only used infrequently by Evagrius, and when he does employ it he does not give to the word any special meaning, but treats it as more or less synonymous with the intellect (*nous*).[34] When Macarius speaks of the heart, on the other hand, he gives to the word the full richness that it possesses in the Bible.[35] For Macarius the heart denotes not merely our emotions and affections but the moral and spiritual centre of the entire human person. The heart is the seat not just of our feelings but of our intelligence and wisdom. We *think* with our heart. The heart is at the same time the region of spiritual encounter. In the heart we come face to face with the spirits of evil, but it is equally the place where we experience the indwelling presence of Christ and the Holy Spirit.

'The heart itself', writes Macarius in characteristically vivid language, 'is but a small vessel; yet dragons are there, and there also are lions. There likewise are poisonous beasts and all the treasures of evil; rough, uneven roads are there, and precipices. But there too is God, the angels, life and the Kingdom, light and the apostles, the heavenly cities and the treasures of grace – all things are there.'[36] Here the heart is clearly being understood in an all-embracing sense. It is a symbol of wholeness and integration, denoting as it does the totality of the human person, regarded as a spiritual subject.

As a focal point and centre of unity, the heart is connected on the one hand with the body and on the other with the intellect. It is at once both a physical organ and the abode of our highest spiritual faculty, the *nous*, and in this way it serves as a place of meeting between them. Elaborating this idea, Macarius states: 'The heart directs and governs the whole bodily organism; and when grace possesses the pastures of the heart, it rules over all the members and the thoughts. For there, in the heart, the intellect abides as well as all the thoughts of the soul and all its hopes. This is how grace penetrates throughout all the parts of the body.'[37] The *nous* within the heart, affirms Macarius, is like the eye within the total body.[38]

From this it is evident that there are important similarities between the 'intellectualism' of Evagrius and the 'cardiac' anthropology of Macarius. Evagrius, as we have seen, sometimes uses 'heart' as an equivalent to 'intellect'. Both Evagrius and Macarius regard the intellect as the highest faculty in the human person. For Evagrius, indeed, it constitutes the real person; in our true essence we are nothing but pure *nous*.

Macarius, more holistic in his perspective, would certainly not agree with this, but he does indeed regard the intellect as the visionary element in the human being, that which gives to our personhood its sense of purpose and direction.

In the light of this, we need to qualify our initial statement that Evagrius emphasizes the intellect, whereas Macarius gives priority to the heart. This is true as far as it goes, but we need to remember the particular sense which Evagrius and Macarius give to these terms. For Evagrius, as already emphasized, the intellect means, not primarily our reasoning brain, but – much more fundamentally – our ability to apprehend spiritual truth through direct, non-discursive insight and contemplative union. For Macarius, as we have now discovered, the heart signifies not just our emotions and feelings but above all our spiritual self-awareness; and as such it includes the intellect within it. There is, therefore, no irreconcilable opposition here between our two witnesses.

Yet, if there is no basic contradiction between the two, there is none the less a clear difference of emphasis. Precisely because Evagrius fails to assign to the notion of the heart the full biblical connotation which it bears in the *Homilies*, Evagrian anthropology lacks the unitary emphasis that is so strikingly evident in Macarius. In the Macarian *Homilies* the heart acts as a symbol of unity, drawing together body, soul and spirit (or intellect), but Evagrius has no such indicator for the wholeness of our threefold personhood.

The difference between the two becomes abundantly plain when their respective theologies of the human body are compared. Because Evagrius, in typically Origenistic fashion, regards the body as extrinsic to true personhood, our human physicality does not play any creative function in his scheme of the spiritual life; our aim is to become simply a 'naked' intellect. Macarius, on the other hand, believes that our objective is nothing less than the transfiguration of the integral human person, body, soul and spirit together. The body is central to his understanding of salvation history. Prior to the fall, the bodies of Adam and Eve were clothed outwardly in glory; after they had sinned, they were deprived of this glory and so they saw themselves as naked.[39] Our reconciliation with God involves a recovery of this primordial glory of the body. Moses foreshadows the ultimate restoration; after his meeting with God on Sinai, when he descended from the mountain his face shone with such radiance that it had to be covered by a veil.[40] Far more significantly, on Mount Tabor the three chosen disciples saw Christ transfigured with bodily glory.[41] The light of the transfiguration on Tabor, as well as looking back to the glory of Adam and Eve at the beginning, also looks forward to the Last Day: it is an eschatological glory. What happened to Christ on Tabor will also happen to the blessed at the final resurrection: 'What the soul now has treasured up within her will be revealed at the Last Day and displayed outwardly ... At the day of resurrection the glory of the Holy Spirit comes out from within, decking and covering the bodies of the saints. This glory they had before, but it was hidden within their souls.'[42]

In all this Macarius is far removed from the Origenism of Evagrius. The *nous* is not isolated from the body but united with it. Macarius is not speaking in these passages with particular reference to the act of praying, but it is obvious what kind of an understanding of prayer follows from this holistic and integrated anthropology. Prayer, as an activity of the heart, must necessarily involve the total person: not the *nous* only but equally the *dianoia*, and also the body with its feelings and its senses. St Paul's approach is equally that of Macarius: 'Your body is a temple of the Holy Spirit ... Glorify God in your body' (1 Cor. 6.19–20); 'Offer your bodies as a living sacrifice, holy and acceptable to God' (Rom. 12.1).

If the body is in no way excluded by Macarius from the work of prayer, then neither is the imagination. Whereas Evagrius has as his ideal a form of prayer that is non-iconic, stripped of images and concepts, there is no such teaching in the *Homilies* of Macarius. These insist upon the need for our prayer to be 'undistracted',[43] but that is as far as they go. Nowhere does Macarius suggest that our prayer should be free not just from wandering and distractive thoughts but from *all* thoughts whatsoever.

In other respects, however, Evagrius and Macarius share much in common. Admittedly, Macarius is more explicitly 'ecstatic' than Evagrius. It sometimes happens, writes Macarius, that 'the inner self is ravished during prayer and plunged into the unfathomable depths of that other world with great sweetness'; in its rapture the intellect becomes oblivious of all earthly concerns and is 'taken captive by things divine and heavenly ... by wonderful things that cannot be expressed in human speech.'[44] Evagrius is more cautious than Macarius in his use of such language, but as we have seen he too believes that at the higher levels of prayer the intellect becomes unaware of its surroundings and even of itself. Here the difference between the two is one of degree, not of basic principle.

Another point of similarity is that Macarius, like Evagrius, speaks on many occasions about visions of light. For both of them, such visions exist on two levels, created and uncreated. The distinction of levels is less clear in Macarius; but he too speaks sometimes about an experience in which the soul sees itself as light,[45] while at other times he refers to visions of 'the light of God' or of 'divine light'.[46] Elsewhere Macarius speaks of union with 'immaterial and divine fire'.[47] In common with Evagrius, Macarius is definitely a 'light' mystic, and nowhere does he speak of the mystical union in terms of darkness.

It would, however, be a mistake to conclude from this emphasis upon divine light that Evagrius and Macarius are non-apophatic in their basic standpoint. In fact both of them insist upon the unknowability of God. In this respect Evagrius is a faithful disciple of the Cappadocians. 'How great is the folly of those who say that they know the nature of God', he writes, in a passage that is clearly directed against the Eunomians.[48] Similarly, Macarius displays a strong awareness of God as mystery. Using an argument *a fortiori*, to be found also in Philo and St Basil the Great, Macarius points out that we do not understand the nature of our own soul; how much less can we understand the nature of God! 'What shall we say? Where is the invisible God to be found? Is he on the earth? Is he in the heavens? Is he beneath the sea? Or under the earth? Who can seize hold of him or catch sight of him? Not a single created thing.' He adds that the unseen God can be grasped by love alone.[49]

Arrow prayers

Let us come to one last question. How far do Evagrius and Macarius propose some practical method whereby we may be

24

assisted to achieve (in the case of Evagrius) non-iconic prayer, and (in the case of Macarius) undistracted prayer? Here the modern reader is likely to feel a certain disappointment, for neither author is much concerned to offer detailed 'techniques'.

St Diadochus of Photice (mid-fifth century), who takes over the teaching of Evagrius concerning prayer as the 'shedding of thoughts', suggests that in order to achieve an image-free state we should practise the continual repetition of the Jesus Prayer:

> When we have blocked all its outlets by means of the remembrance of God, the intellect requires of us imperatively some task which will satisfy its need for activity. For the complete fulfilment of its purpose we should give it nothing but the prayer 'Lord Jesus' ... Let the intellect continually concentrate on these words within its inner shrine with such intensity that it is not turned aside to any mental images.[50]

In this manner the repeated invocation of the Holy Name serves as a 'way in' to non-iconic prayer.

Can we find similar teaching in Evagrius? It seems that we cannot. Nowhere does he recommend the repetition of some short formula – the use of what are often termed 'monologic' or 'arrow' prayers[51] – as a way of stripping the intellect from thoughts and images and bringing it to unity. In his work *On Prayer* he simply says, with reference to demonic attacks, 'At the time of trials such as these, use a brief but intense prayer';[52] but he does not suggest that this 'brief' prayer should be constantly repeated, nor does he link it specifically with the 'shedding of thoughts'. In the *Antirrhetikos* he advises us to repel temptations by using an appropriate biblical text, but once again there is no special emphasis upon the continual repetition of such texts. Still less does Evagrius attribute a special efficacy to the invocation of the Name of Jesus.

What of Macarius? Although for the most part he says little or nothing about practical 'methods', there is one very interesting passage where he recommends the constant repetition of a short formula of prayer: 'Always build up your soul spiritually, and always speak out against the sin that dwells within you, since you have free will; and always pray to God. When you pray, what are you to say? "I beseech you, I beseech you, O Lord." Say these same words alike when walking and when

25

KALLISTOS WARE

eating and drinking, and never cease from doing this.'[53] While there is no reference here to the Name of Jesus, Macarius certainly has in view something closely similar to the 'monologic' prayer of the Desert Fathers of Egypt.

Elsewhere Macarius repeats his injunction that prayer should be as far as possible uninterrupted and continuous, although without mentioning the use of a short formula. 'The Christian ought always to preserve the remembrance of God', he says. 'For it is written, "You shall love the Lord your God with all your heart" (Deut. 6.15). He should love the Lord, not only when he enters the house of prayer, but whether walking or talking or eating he should maintain the remembrance of God and a sense of love and yearning towards him.'[54] Even in the midst of outward distractions, we can continue to pray: 'It may happen that the saints of God sit in the theatre and look at the deception of the world; but in their inner self they are talking with God.'[55] Texts such as this certainly influenced the later development of the Jesus Prayer, even though they themselves make no explicit reference to the Holy Name.

The Cunard Menu

I remember that when I travelled to America on the old *Queen Elizabeth* as a hungry student some forty years ago, the meals were included in the price of the ticket. I found to my delight that the menu in the restaurant was not subdivided into a limited number of courses. Instead of being obliged to choose only one of the various items within each course, we were simply presented with an undifferentiated list of dishes, and we could select as many as we liked. At breakfast we could have both cereals *and* porridge, and then both fried eggs *and* poached haddock (an option I rejected in the heaving waters of the mid-Atlantic). At dinner, however, I used to choose seven courses: *hors d'oeuvre*, soup, fish, meat, dessert, cheese and savoury. The five-day journey passed pleasantly enough.

The catering policy of the Cunard liners may surely be emulated by students of Christian spirituality. Instead of saying either/or, let us say both/and. Instead of choosing between Evagrius and Macarius, let us include both of them on our noetic menu. The two 'currents' that they represent should be seen as complementary rather than mutually exclusive; a balanced theology of prayer has need of both of them. Evagrius requires to be 'de-Platonized' and incorporated in a framework that is more Christocentric in its basic vision and more holistic in its anthropology; his clarity and precision need to be suffused with the affective warmth of the Macarian *Homilies*. But at the same time the enthusiasm of Macarius needs to be moderated by the more systematic approach of Evagrius.

This, indeed, is exactly what happens in the evolution of Eastern Christian spirituality from the fifth century onwards. There is an increasing convergence. The Evagrian terminology and classification are largely retained, but a Macarian content is read into them. This merging of the two 'currents' is to be seen already in the work of St Diadochus of Photice, writing about half a century after Evagrius and Macarius. The 'growing together' continues in St Maximus the Confessor, and then in St Symeon the New Theologian and in the fourteenth-century Hesychasts. In this as in other fields, it is legitimate to speak of a creative 'Byzantine synthesis'.

Notes

1. On Evagrius and Macarius, see Andrew Louth, *The Origins of the Christian Mystical Tradition: From Plato to Denys* (Oxford: Oxford University Press, 1981), pp. 100–125 (bibliography, pp. 208–9); Simon Tugwell, *Ways of Imperfection: An Exploration of Christian Spirituality* (London: Darton, Longman & Todd, 1984), pp. 25–36, 47–58; compare also his contribution to Cheslyn Jones *et alii* (eds), *The Study of Spirituality* (London: SPCK, 1986), pp. 168–75. There are good articles on both authors in the *Dictionnaire de Spiritualité*: on Evagrius, by Antoine and Claire Guillaumont, in vol. 4 (1961), cols 1731–44; on Macarius, by Vincent Desprez, in vol. 10 (1977), cols 20–43. On the relation of the *Homilies* to Messalianism, see Columba Stewart, *'Working the Earth of the Heart': The Messalian Controversy in History, Texts, and Language to AD 431* (Oxford: Oxford University Press, 1991); compare George Maloney's briefer discussion in *Pseudo-Macarius: The Fifty Spiritual Homilies and the Great Letter* (Classics of Western Spirituality; New York/Mahwah: Paulist Press, 1992), pp. 1–33.

2. See Irénée Hausherr, 'Les grands courants de la spiritualité orientale', *Orientalia Christiana Periodica* 1 (1935), pp. 114–38; English translation in *The Eastern Churches Quarterly* 2 (1937), pp. 111–21, 175–85. Hausherr, so it seems, later became dissatisfied with some of the generalizations in this piece, for he did not choose to include it in the two volumes of his collected articles, *Hésychasme et prière* (Orientalia Christiana Analecta 176; Rome, 1966) and *Etudes de spiritualité orientale* (Orientalia Christiana Analecta 183; Rome, 1969).

3. But these terms also occur in Evagrius: see, for example, *On Prayer* 41–42 (42–43); 80.

4. *On Prayer* 3.

5. Ibid., 34a (35), 35 (36).

6. *Republic* VI, 509d–511e.

7. *To Thalassius* 60 (*PG* 90: 624A).

8. *Mystic Treatises by Isaac of Nineveh*, Homily 22, tr. A. J. Wensinck (Amsterdam: Koninklijke Akademie van Wetenschappen, 1923), p. 114; compare *The Ascetical Homilies of Saint Isaac the Syrian*, Homily 23, tr. Holy Transfiguration Monastery (Boston: Holy Transfiguration Monastery, 1984), p. 118. I have slightly adapted Wensinck's version.

9. *On Prayer* 3.

10. Ibid., 66 (67).

11. Ibid., 70 (71).

12. *The Life of Moses* 2:165; cf. Exod. 20.4.

13. *Gnostic Chapters* 1:65; 3:6, 15, 21, etc.

14. *On Prayer* 55 (56), 70 (71), 72 (73), 75 (76), etc.

15. Ibid., 4, 67 (68).

16. Ibid., 114, 115, 117.

17. *Praktikos* 65.

18. *Gnostic Chapters* 4:87.

19. *PG* 12:1644; cf. Tugwell, *Ways of Imperfection*, p. 30.

20. *On Prayer* 120.

21. *Conference* 9:31. For Evagrius' influence on Cassian, see Columba Stewart, *Cassian the Monk* (New York/Oxford: Oxford University Press, 1998), pp. 11–12, 36, *et passim*.

22. *Against Celsus* 3:24; 4:19. Compare *On First Principles* 3:3:4.

23. *Chapters* 9 (*PG* 40:1265B); *On the eight evil thoughts* 9 (*PG* 40:1276A).

24. *On different evil thoughts* (*PG* 40:1244A); *Skemmata* 2, in J. Muyldermans, *Evagriana* (Louvain: Publications Universitaires, 1931), p. 38. At the same time, however, he also speaks of a 'going forth' (*On Prayer* 47) or 'emigration' (*Praktikos* 61) of the

nous towards God; we are 'snatched away' or 'ravished' by *gnosis* (*Praktikos* 66).

25. J. Muyldermans, *Evagriana Syriaca* (Louvain: Publications Universitaires, 1952), p. 164 (§13).

26. See *On Prayer* 5–8, 78.

27. *On Prayer* 66 (67): see above, note 10.

28. *Praktikos* 64.

29. *Gnostikos* 147.

30. *Skemmata* 2, in Muyldermans, *Evagriana*, p. 38. Cf. Exod. 24. 9–11.

31. See the note of John Eudes Bamberger in his translation of Evagrius, *The Praktikos: Chapters on Prayer* (Cistercian Studies Series 4: Spencer, 1970), p. 34, n. 54.

32. *Gnostic Chapters* 2:29.

33. This is also the teaching of Diadochus of Photice, who was influenced by both Evagrius and Macarius: see his work *On Spiritual Knowledge and Discernment: One Hundred Texts* 36.

34. See, for example, *Praktikos* 47.

35. On the meaning of the term 'heart', see A. Guillaumont, 'Les sens des noms du coeur dans l'antiquité', *Le coeur* (Etudes carmélitaines 29; Paris, 1950), pp. 41–81; 'Le "coeur" chez les spirituels grecs à l'époque ancienne', *Dictionnaire de spiritualité*, vol. 2 (1952), cols 2281–8.

36. *Homilies*, Collection II, 43:7.

37. Ibid., II, 15:20.

38. Ibid., II, 43:7.

39. Ibid., II, 12:7–8.

40. Ibid., III, 20:1:3; cf. Exod. 34.29–35.

41. Ibid., II, 15:38.

42. Ibid., II, 5:8–9.

43. See, for instance, ibid., I, 29:1:11; II, 4:4.

44. Ibid., II, 8:1.

45. Ibid., II, 7:5–6 (in this same passage Macarius also mentions 'divine light').

46. Ibid., II, 1:8, 10.

47. Ibid., II, 20:9.

48. *Gnostic Chapters* 5:51; cf. 1:71.

49. *Homilies*, III, 18:1. For the argument that we cannot know our own soul, much less God, compare Philo, *Allegorical Interpretation of the Laws* 1:29 (91)—30 (92); Basil, *Against Eunomius* 1:12 (*PG* 29:540 CD). The same argument appears in Evagrius, *Gnostic Chapters* 2:11; cf. 3:70.

50. *On Spiritual Knowledge and Discernment* 59.

51. See Lucien Regnault, 'La prière continuelle "monologistos" dans la littérature apophtegmatique', *Irénikon* 47 (1974), pp. 467—93. For the idea of 'arrow' prayers, see St Augustine, *To Proba, Ep.* 130:20 (*PL* 33:501), where he says that the 'brethren in Egypt' use prayers that are 'very brief' and 'suddenly shot forth' (*orationes . . . jaculatas*).
52. *On Prayer* 98.
53. *Homilies* I, 6:3:3.
54. Ibid., II, 43:3.
55. Ibid., II, 15:8.

3

FRIENDSHIP

DAVID MOSS

I

Few joys compare with the ecstasy (*ek-stasis*: meaning a standing outside of oneself) of friendship; and few sorrows with its potential agonies. Time spent with friends – a walk, a meal, an unexpected letter – these things make a difference, we could say; perhaps all the difference in the world. But then again, the pain attendant upon a friend's departure or absence – or worse, the torment of a true friend's death – provokes an incalculable tragedy in our lives. Friendship is one, and perhaps one of the profounder measures, of what it means to be human at all. Friendship, claims Adele Fiske, 'is an index of the level of a civilization'.[1]

However, in claiming this, let us make two further observations. The first is this. Friendship quite properly does not yield with any ease to the endeavour of objective description or examination. For sure, we should never take our friends for granted, but then again it would seem that we should never over-burden our friendships with too great a weight of existential expectation and anguish. Friendship is a narrow way which promises entry to the wide expanses of the spirit, but in this promise do we not learn that we should never be too open about our friendships, too prepared to expose them on the rack of objective investigation? In a meditation that fills one with a disturbing recognition, Friedrich Nietzsche remarks of friendship:

[S]uch human relationships almost always depend upon the fact that two or three things are never said or even so much as touched upon: if these little boulders do start to roll, however, friendship follows after them and shatters. Are there not people who would be mortally wounded if they discovered that their dearest friends actually know about them.[2]

Perhaps then, one should barely speak of friendship at all. '*Silentium*,' says Nietzsche. 'One should not talk about one's friends: otherwise one will talk away the feeling of friendship.'[3] Friendship reveals as it retires, illumines as it withdraws. In this, one can say, it is much like love; much like the revelation of love and love of revelation.

However, when these caveats have been registered perhaps we should not be too delicate here. As Francis Bacon would remind us in his famous essay *Of Friendship*, on the verge of friendship we are as 'cannibals' – cannibals ready to consume our own and other hearts. And this, according to St Anselm, and somewhat bizarrely, with that particular organ of friendship: 'the mouth of the heart'. Friendship has no doubt always eaten us up; so then should we understand friendship to be a consumption of sorts? Bacon continues, the man who would be without friendship 'taketh it of the beast, and not from humanity' for 'No receipt openeth the heart but a true friend'.[4] And a weary but still passionate St Augustine would no doubt agree. For looking back on a long and tumultuous life he would reflect: 'what consolation have we in this human society, so replete with mistaken notions and distressing anxieties, except the unfeigned faith and mutual affection of genuine, loyal friends.'[5]

No doubt as we reflect upon the 'modes of human moods' (that index of existence that runs all the way from despair to ecstasy) then friendship may indeed be seen to enjoy a particular power. As Bacon puts it, friendship has 'two contrary effects . . . it redoubleth joys, and cutteth griefs in halfs'. It is little wonder then that such a gift in shortening the abysmal measure of human existence (of halving our descent to despair and in redoubling our ascent towards heaven) has been identified as having something of the sacred, even the divine about it. And in a living and thinking so unfamiliar to us now in which one listened for the play of resonances and sympathies descending through all the gradations of being and so sought to become attuned to the sacred order of the cosmos, friendship was freighted with a divine intensity. It was, in short, interpreted as a way of return to the happiness of paradise. It is this thought that leads on to my second introductory comment. For what of friendship today? What of friendship in an age less impressed by the rigours of an ascent to paradise than by a fascination with the dark and hellish regions of life?

For sure we continue to understand that friendship in many ways makes life worth living. But today the discourse of friendship is 'authorized' by no one and no thing. We have to hand neither a vocabulary which can range over the intellectual and sensual dimensions of friendship nor political ideals that will draw friendship to the centre of the city. More so, friendship seems forsaken by precisely those languages to which it would appear most akin – and most especially 'the language of love'. Thus it appears almost odd to discover that the life of the Irish playwright Samuel Beckett – whose work repeatedly charted the collapse of eloquence into a silence which intimates only aloneness and thereby gives to our age some of its most potent myths – was full of friendship, communication and words.[6] It is not that we do not make friends any more (the suggestion is plain nonsense) but rather that today we experience an absolution from a tradition of friendship which presented its particular bonding, pedagogy, and institutions as central not only to human flourishing but more so to the life of the human spirit in is pilgrimage towards God.[7]

For the Chistian this must surely give pause for thought when, as Nicholas Lash suggests, 'Friendship – and this word can bear so much more weight than we usually seem prepared to put upon it – is the human form that God's love takes.'[8] It is a bold suggestion, but one in which Lash finds himself in good company; in company with a tradition of thinking upon and experiencing friendship that burnt with greater and lesser degrees of intensity in the West between the fourth and twelfth centuries. We may point to, as but the highwater mark of this tradition, the thought of St Aelred of Rievaulx in his *De Spirituali Amicitia*. In this work, written as a dialogue between friends, Aelred's interlocutor Ivo inquires 'Shall I say of friendship what Jesus' friend, the apostle John said of grace, that "God is friendship"?' Aelred replies, 'That would indeed be unusual, and it does not have any scriptural authority. However, I do not hesitate at all to ascribe to friendship that which follows from grace, since (as it were) "he who abides" in friendship "abides in God and God in him".'[9] Clearly we discover here a very high, indeed 'mystical' doctrine of friendship and no mere civic institution for the binding of communities or partnerships together.

The main business of this essay is to recall this remarkable tradition of mystical friendship by pointing to some of its sources and indicating several of its central themes. It is a tradition we can count as running – with no doubt a certain wilful and arbitrary choice here – from Augustine (354–430) to Aquinas (1224/5–1273). Almost inevitably it takes its mark from the impressive fusion achieved by St Augustine in his mediation of Greek and Christian worlds.[10] Continuing on we can see its development through late antiquity in Gregory the Great (540–604) and Benedict (480–550) before discovering a remarkable flowering in the Carolingian period of the eighth/ninth century with whom we associate the name of Alcuin (740–804) in particular. In an eclipse for the following two centuries it is then to the twelfth century that one turns to discover the 'Age of Friendship' which is so closely associated with the monastic experience of Anselm (1033–1109), Bernard of Clairvaux (1090–1153) and Aelred of Rievaulx (1109–67). It is finally Aquinas who brings systematic form to the attention that this tradition took with the windings of the soul in friendship. In his *Summa Theologiae* (II.II.23) he considers the nature of a divinely given friendship which transforms human friendship into *caritas*.

Now in this recounting one is faced with the question of the relationship between the persistent value in a tradition of experience and its contingent manifestations in time. In comparing for example the experience of Augustine in fourth-century Hippo and Anselm in twelfth-century Canterbury, where does one find a common core, if indeed one does? This is not a particularly nuanced way of putting the issue; none the less what I would claim for this tradition, and in large part what makes it so compelling, is its radical fusion of an exquisite attention to the intuitive sense and senses of being human beings in relationship with a rigorous doctrinal commitment to churchly public discourse about the Faith. Friendship is not a private domain to be undisturbed by the very visible and often harsh commitments of Church practice; but nor is doctrine to be understood as a dry theory having little to do with the way that people really live their lives. In other words spirituality and doctrine belong together and this, I suggest, is one way of trying to talk about the persistent value in a historical tradition. In the spirituality of friendship I think we have a privileged view upon what this belonging together can look like.

So then with these preliminary observations made I want to turn now to indicate the sources or tributaries that together run into the mystical conception of friendship that we find developing from Augustine to Aquinas. How was it that the covenanted experience of Israel, or the central political dimension of friendship articulated in Greece and Rome, became, for the Christian imagination of Anselm or Bernard for instance, a central theme in their investigations into the love of God as witnessed to in the incarnation?

II

If we take our lead from the Old Testament what do we discover here? In the first Book of Samuel we come across what has often been seen as one of the most poignant stories in the Hebrew Bible; and one indeed that has provoked much reflection and allegorical interpretation of the experience of friendship in Jewish and Christian traditions. This concerns the unlikely friendship between Jonathan, the king's son, and the future king of Israel, David. The story though must be treated carefully for at its core lies a rather odd if not 'unbalanced' relationship: in point of fact the friendship between Jonathan and David appears to have sprung from nowhere and is told entirely from Jonathan's perspective. Theologically, the narrative points not to that experience of reciprocity that has repeatedly been taken to be the decisive mark of friendship in the tradition, but to friendship as a sort of hermeneutical category deployed in this instance in order to point up the course of salvation history. The relationship recounted has more to do with the protection of David as God's chosen instrument than it does with the experience of friendship itself. None the less it is worth noting that when Saul and Jonathan are killed in battle David will sing these words in his famous lamentation. 'I am distressed for you, my brother Jonathan; very pleasant have you been to me; your love to me was wonderful, passing the love of women' (2 Sam. 1.26 RSV).

In brief, we can suggest that the Old Testament does not deploy friendship as either a central narrative category for telling the story of God's dealings with Israel nor yet as a key hermeneutical concept for characterizing the fundamental relation between the creature and Creator. There are of course exceptions pointing in this direction, and in response to David's 'misogynist' tendencies one could mention the relationship between Ruth and her mother-in-law Naomi, in the book of Ruth. But here again the intention seems to have more to do with the way in which the faithfulness of the daughter-in-law intimates the covenantal faithfulness of God rather than the 'mystical' aspects of friendship.

No doubt covenant and friendship bear a certain analogy, none the less it must be of some note that as far as Israel's meditation upon the nature of life goes the Psalms have very little to say about friendship. For scattered reference one would rather have to look to the wisdom literature.

The Hebrew tradition then uses the word 'friend' and 'friendship' far less often than in Greek and Roman literature and it is therefore to the classical tradition that we need to briefly cast an eye. In the Greco-Roman world friendship was highly valued; it was the most natural thing in the world. Friendship constituted not only a sure foundation for civic life in the *polis*, and, as such, the point of departure for all worthwhile human relationships, but it was also central to a form of Platonic mysticism. For example, in Plato's dialogue the *Phaedros*, it is the love of friends that enables the 'philosophical lover' – literally the one who befriends wisdom – to acquire wings (249A) in the presence of the beloved (251B). And when fully winged his soul soars upwards, attaining again the primeval vision of truth and beauty. Friendship is that 'mania' which transforms us into a 'winged splendour, capable of soaring to the contemplation of eternal verities'.

Two of the most important descriptions of the nature and value of friendship in the tradition are given in Aristotle's *Nichomachean Ethics*, Books 8 and 9, and in the Latin orator Cicero's famous *De amicitia*. Indeed, one could say that Aristotle laid the ground rules for an understanding of friendship in Western civilization.

For Aristotle the most genuine friendship exists between

those who are good and virtuous. Fundamentally friendship is not a private matter nor a psychological enclave. It is rather a type of relationship which constitutes the creation of a good and happy society. The division between public and private, so common to our own imaginations, was simply not part of the 'grammar' of the classical tradition. Little wonder then that considerable hermeneutical demands are placed upon us when we come to try to make sense of texts and traditions that avow the centrality of friendship for all aspects of our lives.

Cicero, the Latin rhetorician, wrote in his *De amicitia*, 'With the single exception of Wisdom, I am inclined to regard [friendship] as the greatest of all the gifts the gods have bestowed on mankind.'[11] His thought had a profound effect on the Middle Ages and most especially on the twelfth century, the so-called 'golden age of friendship'. The Latin root of *amicitia* (friendship) – *amo* – means 'I love'. Friends were ones who loved each other. But this not as a love restricted to our modern accounts of romantic love. Rather this love (what the Greeks called *philia*) was once again central to the good order of the *polis* – the organic political institution. It is Cicero who offered perhaps the most famous definition of friendship: 'complete identity of feeling about all things divine and human, as strengthened by mutual goodwill and affection'.[12]

Thus, if one puts together this idea of friendship as establishing a harmonious politics along with a Platonic influence which, in very rough and ready terms, sought to map community on to an ascending appreciation of being – in other words a discernment of the way in which the world was ordered according to sacred order – then one can fairly easily see how Christianity's concern with both personal salvation and ecclesial existence can find much of value in the classical tradition.

However, when all this is said and done it is to the New Testament that we must turn in order to take our most fundamental orientation; and it is here that the matter becomes considerably more demanding.

At the Last Supper, as recorded in the Gospel of John, Jesus shares with his disciples many things, not least of which is his friendship and reflections thereupon.

This is my commandment, that you love one another as I have loved you. Greater love has no man than this, that a man lay down his life for his friends. You are my friends if you do what I command you. No longer do I call you servants, for the servant does not know what his master is doing; but I have called you friends, for all that I have heard from my Father I have made known to you (John 15.12–15 RSV)

The words of Jesus here offer no counsel of conviviality, no Ciceronian discernment of shared or harmonious interests as it were. But nor do they promise anything less than real friendship – a personal encounter with the Other. For after all, this man had entertained friendships with others: with Lazarus, John, Mary, Martha. Rather we must understand that if friendship is to find a place within the Christian economy at all then it is destined to find residency in the commandment to love. Something like, we could suggest: love me, love one another, obey me. And here is surely the greatest tension. For the commandment to love, and the obedience it entails, is unyielding.

This, one could claim, is the charter for Christian existence and we should be clear that it takes no heed of our human potential for observing it. All that is important is that it is observed; this marks its character as a commandment. Now one would surely want to say that if we take heed to obey, then God will not fail to give us the means to do so. But one thing he will not do and that is to accommodate his commandment to human insufficiency. For there is only one thing that love cannot endure and that is to have limits set upon it. Under this commandment, this objective logic of love so to speak, love cannot be perceived as any penultimate good for our spirit or city. We cannot reserve for it any circumscribed place in our soul, or assign to it a limited portion of our strength. This love, God's love, is nothing other than self-giving and therefore has no other law than itself. Henceforth, all other laws are to be subsumed under it.

Now this may sound dangerously strident. It may sound a bit like this I admit, and what I have said could do with a good deal of theological unpacking, nevertheless my intention here is to make a fundamental theological point about the spirituality of friendship.

For sure, the co-ordinates of reference for understanding what friendship is and the purpose it plays must in some way remain in any Christian appropriation of the sources we have just described. Friendship may operate as a distant analogy to God's covenantal relationship; friendship may function as a civic, political or even ecclesial cement; it may even fuel an impassioned (in Plato's terms, erotic) ascent towards the ideas, or ideals of truth, goodness and beauty. However, in the 'Christian dispensation' these aspects are all now radically reorientated in this world of a new commandment. For they are henceforth to be co-ordinated within the commandment to love. Friendship is as it were to be redirected towards the incarnational movement of God – what the tradition has called God's kenotic self-giving or self-emptying love. Oddly then, paradoxically even, this movement which promises us our freedom and creativity comes upon us as command precisely because love, God's love, knows no limit.

Moreover, if we can talk about a spirit of love we can see, from another perspective, why we need to be careful in our use of the term 'spirituality' in Christian theology. And this because, whatever spirituality names in the Christian tradition, it most assuredly does not name a domain, private and partial, of an inner psychic reality fed by appropriate therapeutic techniques. Rowan Williams has suggested that to live in the Spirit is to live a whole human life in a certain direction; which is to say a human life 'performed' in the context of a set of relations determined by the commandment to love. It is the cultivation and nourishing of this entire set of relations that provides the fuel for our movement in the Spirit; that, so to speak, gives us a directionality through life. In the terms I have just used, if what is important about the commandment to love is that it is obeyed, then how it is to be obeyed is where spirituality finds its proper place.

Now if we follow this description of what the tradition understands by living lives in the Spirit of Christ, then we can see why friendship and life in the Spirit enjoy a sort of 'elective affinity'. For both pivot upon the reality of stories or narratives of human, even divine being as dynamic, relational, self-giving, poured out, and in some sense destined towards unity and communion. The Christian life involves many aspects but central to its reality and its meaning is the overcoming, or living beyond the isolation that both our finitude and our sinfulness imposes upon us. In more theological language, this is indicated in the ancient and generative christological *pro me* formula. Christ died for me. To exist or to be is for the human being to become; moreover it is to become for another in imitation of the one who became flesh, became servant for me. We are to become ourselves for God and for neighbour. If this is so then perhaps we can better see the attraction of privileging friendship as a most appropriate characterization of Christian life.

But how are we to understand friendship under the law of love – as radically kenotic? As no mere civic glue, nor covenantal proxy but as the human being's participation in the triune life of God? This, it strikes me, is where the tradition of spiritual or mystical friendship becomes a most compelling guide for precisely the reason that it illuminates aspects of the generative source of the Christian tradition itself: a living under the commandment of love.

What the evidence of, for example, the monks of the twelfth century suggests is that they were sure that they themselves and their friends were images of the living God, that their mutual love was real, and that in their friendships they became most themselves. They may have been deluded of course; however, they may offer us a demonstrably deeper penetration into the fundamental narrative of the Christian Church: an obedience to the law of love. It is in a brief attempt to try and explain what this involves here that I now want to turn to three themes which recur repeatedly in the mystical tradition of friendship from Augustine through to Aquinas. We can view these themes as parts of a sort of grammar for this type of relationship called friendship.

III

The three themes are as follows:

- Recognition: the recognition of a likeness or similitude in the friend. I 'find' myself in you (the Other) in Christ.

- The Sensual: this discovery or recognition occurs through an experience of the convolution of the senses, an 'emptying' of our senses into one another.
- The Intellectual: the provocation of an intellectual ascent, a *theoria*, in which the human mind trembles into a contemplation of the goodness, truth and beauty of God.

Now as a preliminary indication as to what this grammar of mystical friendship adds up to we can suggest the following. In response to the movement of incarnation – the self-giving of the Father in the Word become flesh – a corresponding movement is demanded from and offered to the creature: the Creator's condescension is met in the ascension of the creature. The occasion for this recognition and 'movement' is friendship. For not only is this experience taken to be profoundly religious but, more, it is essentially Christian (and not the mere impersonal 'touch' of the divine) in that it introduces one through the Other into the relationship of persons articulated in the two great mysteries of the Trinity and incarnation. Human persons ascend in a mystical movement from the scene of human friendship – of loved and beloved – by way of the participation in Word – or image of the invisible God – towards Trinitarian life. I will consider each aspect of this movement in turn.

1. To take our bearings from Augustine, the goal of friendship in Christ is the union of souls in possession of God, a finding of one another and oneself in tranquillity and security. Friendship begins in a mutual attraction but its testing for Augustine lies far beyond the sharing of mutual interests or the accidental and occasional joint endeavour. The mutual attraction of friendship springs from the recognition of a similitude. Classically, like recognizes like, or what I recognize in a friend is me in you in God. The friend is really recognized as my alter ego such that Augustine is able to write to Jerome that he sees him through the eyes of his friend Alypius; for 'so great is the union of heart, so firm the intimate friendship subsisting between us'.[13] In difficult language there is here an 'ontological' recognition, which is to say a recognition at the most fundamental level of created being. And what I recognize in you and so in me – for in you I recognize me – is the image of God.

Now at this point we would need to move into a rich theology of the *imago dei*, something that is beyond us here. None the less, what we should seek to understand in order to grasp Augustine's intention, and indeed the transfiguration of friendship in Christ, is the christological meaning of the *imago dei* – that, according to 2 Cor. 4.4, Christ is image or icon of the invisible God. To recognize in the friend the image of God and so oneself is not to recognize a picture of myself (a Polaroid snapshot) in a little mirror installed in you by God. Rather, what is at issue here is a christological recognition; a discovery of my 'self' being poured out in you in love as you in me. And this as our common participation in the pouring out of the Son from the Father. The very physicality, or bodiliness, of the analogy here is important, if not at times troubling. The language and images that pervade the letters and words exchanged between friends in this tradition are often highly charged and erotic. They present us perhaps with a poetics of friendship which seeks to be adequate to that vertigo often experienced in love and friendship. However, they can do this only so long as they remain rigorously anchored in an account of the meaning of the image of God in us. At stake here is the recognition, through friendship, of oneself and the other in and through the very movement of God's condescension, of his love for the world.

2. However, if the similitude I discover in friendship is the discovery of myself in the image of God in you (and vice versa) then for Augustine and the tradition that follows him, this identification or recognition is physically marked in the experience of *dulcitudo* or sweetness.[14] The experience is ineffable, hidden, but overwhelming. There is an excessive sensual experience associated with this recognition of the image in the friend as indeed this sweetness can and will become the occasion for an acute pain at its passing. This is what I shall call the convolution of the senses: the way in which a seeing or hearing of a friend becomes a sensing or feeling of the friend in their presence or absence. It is a movement particularly evidenced in the friendships of St Anselm. Let me give but one extended example from his letters:

But what of this that neither eye has seen nor ear heard but only into the heart of man has it entered ... My witness is the experience of my consciousness, that the taste of this affection is not perceived by any sight or hearing, save inasmuch as it is conceived in the mind of each. Since therefore that you know that the sweetness of love is recognised, neither by eyes nor ears, but tasted delightfully by the mouth of the heart, with what words or letters shall my love and yours be described? Let our own consciousness suffice for us, by which we are conscious to each other of how much we love each other.[15]

Let us put it like this. In the interiorization of the image in friendship what I come to hold, to behold, to taste, is the image of the one who holds my image. This is the acute mutuality of friendship according to Anselm. In the friend I see me; in me I see the friend – and it is this I taste. Perhaps it is worth remembering that it is at a meal shared between friends – the *caritas christiani* of the Last Supper – that eternal truth is not so much sighted as tasted and consumed. Clearly attention given to reading, discerning or tasting these 'sensual' experiences is part and parcel of what the tradition sees is involved in true spiritual recognition: the recognition of the grammar of our own sensual convolutions learnt through friendship.

3. Finally, we should recognize that in the mystical tradition friendship becomes the occasion or scene for an intellectual or theoretic ascent towards God. In a most remarkable passage which demands considerable exegesis Augustine writes: 'Commune with your own soul, and raise it up, as far as you are able, unto God. For in him you hold us also by a firmer bond, not by means of bodily images, which we must meanwhile be content to use in remembering each other, but by means of that faculty of thought through which we realize the fact of our separation from each other.'[16]

If we have touched upon recognition and sweetness in friendship, this quotation points to my third theme and that is the ascent of thought; of what is called in the tradition *theoria* (theory) and which is now so badly understood as a rather dry, if not useless activity. However, in the spiritual tradition *theoria* names the transfiguration of thought itself, the direct meditation of the human praying mind upon the goodness, truth and beauty of God, in God's self. What the mystical tradition of friendship gives evidence of is the fact that the highest capacity of the intellect to meditate upon God is generated from the scene or occasion of friendship. Truest thought, the most radical movement of the intellect, is nothing but the most radical power of love itself – love for the Other. To make friends and make sense are similar activities, we can suggest. Thus, to make true friends and true sense are therefore of necessity conjoined. Moreover in this ascent, thought is not destined to disappear in a dissolution effected by the emptiness of God. Thought does not expire in a dark night in which all cats are black; a sort of Zen-inspired nothingness. This is not the meaning of the *via negativa*. Contemplation of God involves the transfiguration and not collapse of our created powers. And why? For precisely the reason that the friend is not lost in the Absolute, nor left behind as a step in the ascent. And why again? Because finally, Jesus Christ – the image of God and divine friend – can never be left behind or abandoned as a step towards God.

It is hardly novel to claim that Augustine – and the tradition that followed him – transformed the ideas he received from the classical world; nor even that the world of Christendom is at one level a history of what happened to his ideas. None the less this reality and transformation can be particularly well seen in the context of friendship.

For sure the Christian tradition inherited elements of ancient friendship as a necessary social glue for political and civic life – the practical forms of friendship which continued to influence Christianity through Jerome, Boniface and Bernard with its emphasis on mutual duties and harmonious living. However, a spiritualized understanding of friendship with deep roots in Platonic theology is also plainly evident, and comes to fruition in the tradition we have been considering – likeness between friends, interior presence, an ascending *theoria*. All this is carried into Augustine's thought and vision. But in the new world of the incarnate Word, the commandment to love, all this is changed and this for the reason that if human beings have never been bereft of the scattered materials that will enable them to build a ladder back to the heavens, it only becomes possible now, after God has first come to us in his Christ. And this as the divine friend.

IV

To conclude: if in the ancient world friendship had always been prized as a social, political and economic necessity, the Church's meditation upon the mystery of the incarnation likewise deepened its understanding of the gift of friendship. In the flowering of this tradition of mystical friendship, from the fourth to the twelfth centuries, we can discern that critical and ancient catholic principle that the possession of God never destroys the appetite for created goodness but rather enhances it. Friendship was revelatory and gifting, a mediation of the divine life into our creaturely condition, in precisely these ways. It gives being in that it becomes the occasion for a recognition that human beings exist fully only in relation to others, and that to love is to admit that another exists. It gives self-knowledge in that the joyful but sometimes severe and rigorous demands of friendship keep one close to the nature of reality as resistant and difficult, as always requiring our labour and patience. And it gives hope because the likeness one encounters in a recognition of the other involves a recognition of God in them – what has traditionally been called the *imago Dei*. The union between friends thus promises a restoration of Eden's peace and, more, a foretaste of the heavenly paradise.

Clearly the history of Christianity provides a profusion of patterns for following Christ, a fact that should absolve us from the prejudice of regarding any one way as determinative and final.

Moreover, that certain patterns seem to become very influential at particular times is also clearly the case. No doubt we should recognize that the privilege given to friendship in, say, Augustine or Gregory can in some part be attributed to a cultural context and social position that taught them that friendship was a good thing; and a philosophical tradition in which friendship had received the imprimatur of no less a figure than Aristotle. All this may be so. However, in an age which can find little place for the virtue of friendship in political existence or a poetry of relationship outside of the acid reductions of sexual attraction, can we still ask 'Whither the tradition of mystical friendship today?'

There is no doubt that any answer to this question would demand a far deeper investigation, both historical and theological alike. It is however an investigation that I believe, for very many reasons, is of considerable importance to us today.

Notes

1. Adele Fiske, *Friends and Friendship in the Monastic Tradition* (Cuernavaca: Centro Intercultural de Documentacion, 1970) 20/1.
2. Friedrich Nietzsche, *Human, All Too Human*, tr. R. J. Hollingdale (Cambridge: Cambridge University Press, 1996), Vol. I, para. 376.
3. Ibid., para. 252.
4. Francis Bacon, 'Of Friendship', *Essays*, introduction by Michael J. Hawkins (London: Dent, 1972), pp. 80–1.
5. *City of God*, Bk XIX, ch. 8.
6. Thus Beckett's long time companion and eventually wife, Suzanne Deschevaux-Dumesnil, once remarked in exasperation, 'Sam fait des copains comme des chiens font des chiots' (Sam makes friends like a dog makes puppies). James Knowlson, *Damned to Fame – The Life of Samuel Beckett* (London: Bloomsbury, 1997), p. 491.
7. See the difficult although important work by Jacques Derrida, *Politics of Friendship*, tr. George Collins (London: Verso, 1997).
8. Nicholas Lash, *The Beginning and the End of 'Religion'* (Cambridge: Cambridge University Press, 1996), p. 43.
9. Aelred of Rievaulx, *Spiritual Friendship*, tr. Mark F. Williams (London: University of Scranton Press, 1994), I. 69–70.
10. See Caroline White, *Christian Friendship in the Fourth Century* (Cambridge: Cambridge University Press, 1992), Ch. 11.
11. Cicero, *On the Good Life*, tr. Michael Grant (London: Penguin Classics, 1971), p. 187.
12. Ibid.
13. Augustine, Letter XXVIII, 1. *The Nicene and Post-Nicene Fathers*, Vol. 1, St Augustine (Edinburgh: T & T Clark, 1994).
14. Augustine, *Confessions* I, 4.
15. Quoted in Fiske, *Friends and Friendship*, 15/12.
16. Augustine, Letter IX, 1. *The Nicene and Post-Nicene Fathers*, Vol. 1, St Augustine.

4

THE ENGLISH MYSTICS

BENEDICTA WARD

> I dreamt a marvellous dream; I was in a wilderness I could
> not tell where ... and between the tower and the gulf I saw
> a smooth field full of folk, high and low together (William
> Langland, *Piers Plowman*, 1332–1400).

The tower of truth and the gulf of sorrow: and between them a
field full of folk. Langland's vision of Piers Plowman is
concerned with the folk between these two extremes, and in
some ways this is a true vision of the fourteenth century itself.
There is always a dynamic unity between the content of a faith
(the 'tower of truth') and the way it is lived out ('the gulf of
sorrow') not by a special élite but by the 'folk' themselves. Spirituality cannot be seen as a pure intellectual stream of
consciousness flowing from age to age among the articulate
people only; it is always the lens of the gospel placed over each
age, each place, each person. The fourteenth century was a
time when it is especially impossible to understand religious
and spiritual matters without reference to the events of the
world in which they were set, so I shall begin our exploration
of the English mystics with some plain background history.

This was a time when serious minded people everywhere
criticized formalism and hypocrisy in religion, especially
among the established religious orders; dissent from orthodoxy
seemed to be in the air, and the most vigorous understanding of
Christian life seemed to be found outside the formal structures
of the Church. It is possible to see the fourteenth century as a
time of widening gaps, with on the one hand a highly efficient
administration in the Papacy, internationally efficacious, with
a minute and detailed code of common and church law,
precise doctrinal formulations issuing from lively debate in the
universities, and an organized, perhaps over-organized, clergy.
There was the tower, concerned with truth and reason; and in
the thirteenth century, especially in England, some strands in

47

theology emerged which were both clarifying and revolutionary. The chief promoters of these new ways of thought were John Duns Scotus and William of Occam, both born in Britain, Franciscans and university men. Their emphasis on love as opposed to knowledge, and the stress on the individual, were to influence, however indirectly and obliquely, the spirituality of the following century and the understanding of the folk around the tower, in their emphasis on love and in the growth everywhere of independent personal piety, literate in the vernacular languages and deeply versed in the Scriptures, involved in lay life rather than monasticism. Sometimes this vigour took the form of heresy, and in England this was most usually called Lollardy.

Whatever truth there may be in this picture – and there could be criticism of it at every point – the other side of it is surely one of great and orthodox vitality, whether issuing in mysticism and piety or in robust criticism of hypocrisy wherever it was found. In fourteenth-century England, there are instances of a new life of Christian piety and it produced written works of the first importance. Perhaps this vigour below the tower of truth was also a reaction to the gulf of sorrow, for this was a century also of overwhelming disaster.

First there was the Hundred Years War, a series of wars between England and France, 1337–1453, arising out of the claims of Edward III to the French crown as grandson of Philip IV, a dynastic clash of Plantagenet and Valois. It affected the lives of thousands apart from the protagonists at the top. At the English victory of Crecy in 1346 French cavalry were decimated by Welsh bowmen, and the Black Prince laid siege to Calais in 1356. At Poitiers again the French cavalry was destroyed. The effects of such clashes were not only in loss of life; there was also an economic consequence: the wool trade in Flanders suffered from the blockades, affecting all concerned in the rising trade within the towns. These brutal wars, reaching a turning point in the next century with Joan of Arc (1433), caused widespread distress both in France and England. Philip de Mézières, a former knight and crusader who had become a hermit, wrote in 1395 what he called 'the letter of an old solitary to king Richard II' insisting that destruction had been spiritual as well as physical:

All have been brought so tragically to the destruction of soul and body by this war ... how many churches by the venom of this wound have been destroyed, how many orphans and widows created who die by hunger and ill treatment. Faith too is in large measure forgotten and destroyed.[1]

In 1380 taxation provoked the Peasants' Revolt, a symptom of widespread unrest, not unconnected with the rise of towns and decay of countryside, but the great gulf of sorrow was connected most of all with the series of plagues called the Black Death. In about 1346 news began to circulate in Europe of horrific events in Far Cathay, that is in China. The dead of a strange disease were being counted in the millions; through trade routes the plague spread to the ports of Constantinople, Venice, Genoa and took firm grip on Sicily. Soon it was in England, an island where it spread rapidly; it was almost always fatal. In the ensuing years one third of the population of Europe died. It was a disease that struck without warning, against which there was no defence and which killed horribly and swiftly with no respect for social status, age or occupation.

> Sceptre and crown
> must tumble down
> and in the dust be equal made
> with the poor crooked scythe and spade.

Such disasters provoked rising hysteria as one episode of the plague died down only to come back again and again. Its aftermath was shattering in social terms and in religion it produced on the one hand a deep concentration on the inner life, and on the other within a context which associated disaster with punishment for man's sin, a sense that established religion had failed to prevent what could be seen as an impartial and unjust damnation; it produced questioning about a God who was love and the blame that he seemed to have unjustly administered.

It is with this background of light and dark, of the folk between the tower and the gulf, that I now turn to the works of five writers known as the English mystics. They do not form a really cohesive group in themselves; they did not know each other or read each other's works, nor were they all 'mystics' in any but the fundamental sense of those concerned with the mystery of God; but all wrote in English, all lived in the fourteenth century in England, and all were in some way concerned with prayer and with solitude. One other part of prayer to be kept in mind when examining personal prayer is the liturgy; the framework of public prayer always provides the basis of personal and private prayer, and in the fourteenth and fifteenth centuries it is noticeable that many of the festivals newly introduced into the corporate public prayer of the Church echo the ideas and devotions of these writers. First, I will introduce the writings of three men who wrote mainly to direct others in the ways of prayer and then those of two women who implemented such instruction in their lives.

Richard Rolle 1290–1349

There were a great number of hermits in England in the fourteenth century. Many remain unknown, some are known mainly by their names such as John de Lacy, a Dominican hermit in Newcastle-under-Lyme; Bartholomew of Farne; John Clapton; Ralph Dyncourt; Hugh Hermit; Lorretta of Hackington; Alice de Beaucourtys; Juliana Lampret. But the best known in his own times was Richard Rolle of Hampole, the Yorkshire hermit. He wrote in Latin and English, and several of his works were for an anchoress called Margaret. He is the only one of the five to be canonized and was commemorated after his death in at least local calendars, under the title 'blessed', with a feast day, a mass and an office. A prolific writer and preacher, he was well known and popular during his life.

Richard Rolle was born at Thornton in Yorkshire, went to the schools in Oxford but left early, apparently dismayed at the aridity of the curriculum, and became a hermit on his own in Yorkshire. His main works were *The Fire of Love*, and *The Emending of Life*. He also wrote a new kind of poetry in his English religious lyrics which have a key place in vernacular literature. Of his influence on English literature there is no doubt, but commentators have been more cautious about his theology and spirituality, however popular it was. He was seen as an exponent of affective mysticism, advising a dependence on sensible feelings in prayer, especially what he called heat, sweetness, and song (*calor, dulcor, canor*). He described it in an autobiographical way:

> In the beginning of my conversion, I thought that I would be like the little bird that languishes for love of his beloved but is gladdened in his longing when he that it loves comes, and sings with joy and in its song languishes in sweetness and heat. It is said that the nightingale is given to song and melody all night that she may please him to whom she is joined. How much more should I sing with great sweetness to Christ my Jesus that is a spouse of my soul through all this present life that is night in regard to the clearness that is to come, so that I could languish in longing and die of love.[2]

Rolle's works reflect many of the main themes of the four-teenth century: he rejected the learning of the university as an arid and barren tower of truth, though, perhaps ironically, his emphasis on love made him the heir of the great Franciscan men of the universities of the previous century, in their assertion that God is reached not by knowledge but by love. He often said that true prayer could never be found in another false tower, that is, any monastery. He lived as a hermit, in the woods, and as well as being a popular and passionate preacher he was a guide to other solitaries. He seems to be an advocate of a positive mysticism but with his image of the soul as a nightingale, he shows that this was no easy way of light:

> But the soul that is in the third degree is all burning fire and like the nightingale that loves song and melody, and dies for great love; so that the soul is only comforted in loving and praising God, and till death comes, is singing in spirit to JESU, and in JESU, and JESU, not bodily, not crying with the mouth, (of that manner I do not speak, for both good and evil have that song.) One thing I tell you, it is of heaven and God gives it to whom He will, but not without great grace coming before. Whoever has it, he thinks all the song and all the minstrelsy of earth naught but sorrow and woe compared thereto.[3]

The darkness of the night in which the nightingale sings has its link with the gulf of sorrow; the folk must pass through this darkness, and sing. He was also a powerful advocate of devotion to the name of Jesus which was finding its reflection also in the new feast of the Name of Jesus (7 August) established in 1457 and in the other new feast of the Transfiguration (6 August) and the feast of the Icon of the Saviour (1449). His writing is at its most lyrical when he considers the name of Jesus:

> Then your soul is Jesu loving, Jesu thinking, Jesu desiring, only in your desire of Him breathing: to Him singing, of Him burning, in Him resting. Then the song of loving and of love has come; then your thought turns into song and into melody; then it is right for you to sing the psalms which before you said; then you must take longer about fewer psalms. You will think death sweeter than honey for then you are quite sure to see Him whom you love. Then you may boldly say: 'I languish for love' and 'I sleep and my heart waketh'.[4]

Rolle has not yet been thoroughly assessed as a theologian, but he remains a very attractive writer and poet. His special genius is shown best in his religious lyrics, written in the style of the lyrics of courtly love but linked with the growing personal devotion to the name of Jesus:

> Hail Jesu, my creator, of sorrowing, medicine;
> Hail Jesu, my saviour that for me suffered pain;
> Hail Jesu, help and succour, my love be aye thine;
> Hail Jesu, the blessed flower of thy mother virgin.[5]

Walter Hilton c. 1343–96

Unlike Rolle, Walter Hilton belonged to a religious order, not of the monastic type but the clerical order of Augustinian canons. He was attached to the priory at Thurgarton in Lincolnshire, though he may have lived as a hermit for a time and his writings were concerned with others in the solitary life. Like so much spiritual writing he says it was done at the request of others, in this case an anchoress. He wrote to his 'spiritual sister in Jesus Christ' with advice she had asked for about prayer and spiritual life, drawing on his own experience to do so. He presented a firm and clear picture of the whole life of

prayer, carefully arranged, set out with gentleness and tolerance though with the austere theme of the mystics: in order to
reach the vision of peace, Jerusalem, one must go through
what he called the 'night of murk':

> For whoso ween for to come to the working and the full use of
> contemplation and not by this way, that is for to say not (by
> the steadfast mind of the precious manhood and the passion
> of Jhesu Christ nor) by fullhead of virtue, he cometh not by
> the door ... For Christ is the door and He is the porter and
> without his life and livery may there no man come in. That
> is for to say, no man may come to the contemplation of the
> Godhead but he first be reformed by fullhead of meekness
> and charity to the likeness of Jhesu in His manhood.[6]

The centre for Hilton in the life of one who prays was Christ
in his passion; the night of murk, the gulf of sorrow, was to be
endured with Christ on the cross in order to come to the light
of truth. He seems to have been critical of the affective mysticism of Rolle and advised against dependence on feeling heat,
sweetness and song in themselves. 'Hearing of delectable song
or feeling of comfortable heat in the body, or seeing of light, or
sweetness of bodily savour ... These are not ghostly feelings ...
but when they are best and most true yet are they but outward
tokens of the inly grace that is felt in the mights of the soul.'[7]

His teaching reflects that of Anselm of Canterbury in what
amounts to a paraphrase of Anselm's preface to his *Prayers and
Meditations*, that turning point in devotion, four centuries
earlier:

> Lo, I have told thee a little as me thinketh, first of contempla-
> tive life what it is, and then of the ways by which grace leads
> thereto. Not that I have it in feeling and working as I have
> it in saying; nevertheless I would by these words such as
> they are, first stir mine own negligence for to do better than
> I have done and also my purpose is for to stir thee or any
> other man or woman that have the state of life contemplative
> for to travail more busily and more meekly in that manner
> of life by such simple words as God hath given me grace for
> to say. And therefore if any word be therein that stirreth or
> comforteth thee more to the love of God, thank God, for it is

His gift and not of the word. And if it comforteth thee not or else thou taketh it not readily, study not too long thereabout; but lay it beside thee for another time, and give thee to thy prayer or to other occupation. Take it as it will come, or not all at once. Also these words that I write take them not too strictly, but there that thee thinketh by good advisement that I speak too shortly ... I pray thee mend it only where need is. Also these words that I write to thee, they long not all to a man which hath active life, but to thee or any other which hath the state of life contemplative.[8]

Deeply biblical and meditative, in some ways Hilton presents the most complete programme for the spiritual life of them all.

The Cloud of Unknowing

In spite of many speculations, the author of *The Cloud of Unknowing* is, perhaps providentially, entirely unknown to us; so even the dates when he wrote are approximate and any influences or contacts are mostly guesswork. He says that he wrote the *Cloud* in English for a young correspondent and it was soon translated into Latin and circulated very widely. He seems from the text to have been well educated in the schools and to have known some of the work on emerging science at Oxford. A man of quick observation and incisive language and perception, he provided an example of the apophatic way of prayer in English, following the tradition of Evagrius, Gregory of Nyssa and Pseudo Dionysius; he knew the *Mystical Theology* of Pseudo Dionysius in a Latin translation and as well as referring to him by name in the *Cloud* he also translated his small treatise into English under the title *Deonise Hid Divinite*. The most brilliant and original of all these writers, the anonymous author of *The Cloud of Unknowing* wrote six or seven other related pieces, some very short, the most important of which is *The Book of Privy Counsel*. He wrote in an East Midlands dialect, probably in the mid-fourteenth century, addressed to a young man of 24 who may have been a Carthusian monk, perhaps at Beauvale, and who was now living as a hermit; he had asked the *Cloud* author for advice about what he was experiencing in prayer. It is important to see that this work is in answer to someone who had already had experiences in prayer which he needed to understand; it is not a new way of prayer that was being taught from the start but the elucidation of existing experience. It was written for one person, and the author insists that it is not to be read generally but only by those called to it. Since it was not for beginners, the author assumes the customary life of the devout person in medieval England and the discipline and the single determination of a life undertaken wholly for prayer as a hermit.

The central image the author used was that of two clouds, the cloud of unknowing and the cloud of forgetting:

> During this exercise, all creatures and all the works of creatures, past, present or future, must be hid in the cloud of forgetting. If ever you come to this cloud, and live and work in it as I bid you, just as this cloud of unknowing is above you, between you and your God, in the same way you must put beneath you a cloud of forgetting, between you and all the creatures that have ever been made. It seems to you, perhaps, that you are very far from him, because this cloud of unknowing is between you and your God. However, if you give it proper thought, you are certainly much further away from him when you do not have the cloud of forgetting between you and all the creatures that have ever been made. Whenever I say 'all the creatures that have ever been made' I mean not only the creatures themselves, but also all their works and circumstances. I make no exceptions, whether they are bodily creatures or spiritual, nor for the state or activity of any creature, whether these be good or evil. In short, I say that all should be hid under the cloud of forgetting.[9]

There is here a clear and decisive personality, full of wit and acute observation, with no time or patience for the sentimental and hypocritical. Writing a racy English prose style, he has a single theme, a clear message, and he delivers it with wisdom, patience and confidence. He insists that true prayer means an increase of love, which reaches further than knowledge and leads into a new way of understanding, in response to a specific call of God: 'Know right well that although I bid thee thus plainly and boldly set thee to this work nevertheless yet I feel verily that Almighty God with his grace must always be the chief stirrer and worker either with means or without and thou only but the consenter and sufferer.'[10]

Like Hilton, the *Cloud* author was dubious about emotional and affective experience: 'All other comforts, sounds and gladness and sweetness that come from without suddenly thou knowest not whence I pray thee have them suspect.'[11] He gives classic teaching about the temptation to follow distracting thoughts in prayer:

> when thou feelst thou mayest in nowise put them down, cower then down under them as a caitiff and coward overcome in battle, and yield thyself to God in the hands of thine enemies ... and this meekness deserves to have God himself mightily descending to avenge thee of thine enemies so as to take thee up and cherishingly dry thy ghostly eyes as the father doth his child that is on the point of perishing under the mouths of wild swine or mad biting bears.[12]

He was not concerned with darkness in a negative or world-denying sense but as a way of freedom, by leaving the obsessiveness of self for the freedom of God: for him, silence of the mind was a way of being able to begin to receive the knowledge of God; it was not an end in itself:

> For silence is not God, nor speaking is not God, fasting is not God nor eating is not God, loneliness is not God nor company is not God, nor any of all such contraries. He is hid between them and may not be found by any work of the soul but only by the love of thine heart. He may not be known by reason, he may not be thought, gotten or traced by understanding. But he may be loved and chosen by the true loving will of thine heart. Choose thee him.[13]

Like Bonaventure and Duns Scotus, the *Cloud* author insists that it is love and not knowledge that leads to God: 'He can be loved but not thought.'

There are no obvious liturgical parallels with this writer but he wrote from the heart of solitary and contemplative prayer and he wrote for the folk on the basis of love, addressing a non-university, non-Latinate and a young audience, which was to be encouraged to go through the darkness of the gulf of sorrow and to find it a place of mercy and of hope:

Take good gracious God as He is, plat and plain as a plaster, and lay it to thy sick self as thou art and try by desire to touch good gracious God as he is. Step up then stoutly and taste that treacle.[14]

Not what thou art, nor what thou hast been seeth God with his merciful eyes but what thou wouldest be.[15]

Margery Kempe 1373–post-1433

Margery Kempe is in some ways the most interesting of the group because the most typical of her age; she is certainly one of the folk busy on the plain. Born at King's Lynn in Norfolk, *c.* 1373, she married John Kempe in 1393, and had fourteen children. A severe mental illness followed the birth of her first child during which she had a vision of Christ and thereafter regarded herself as particularly bound to him by devotion. It was not until 1418, however, when she was 45, that she left home and undertook a life of pilgrimage, accompanied by visions and ecstatic experiences. These were dictated by her (she could not read or write), forming *The Book of Margery Kempe*, the first autobiography in English. It has survived virtually in only one manuscript, which was only recognized as such in 1934. Of immense interest for the history of popular religion, her life and work illuminate some aspects of Christian theology and prayer.

Margery was not a hermit but lived an independent and in a sense non-institutional life, and above all she wept – her cryings were the thing for which she was most famous and for which in her own time she was also criticized:

And this creature had great compunction, with plentiful tears and much loud and violent sobbing for her sins and for unkindness towards her creator ... her weeping was so plentiful and so continual that many people thought that she could weep and leave off when she wanted and therefore many people said she was a false hypocrite and wept when in company for advantage and profit.[16]

She did not find a life of prayer easy but was aware of her need for help to detach herself from dependence upon worldly goods and concerns:

And all manner of worldly goods and dignities, and all manner of loves on earth, I pray you, Lord, forbid me, especially all those loves and possessions of any earthly thing which would decrease my love towards you, or lessen my merit in heaven. And all manner of loves and goods which you know in your Godhead should increase my love towards you, I pray you, grant me for your mercy to your everlasting worship.[17]

Margery was in the tradition of devout women mystics such as Hildegard of Bingen, Catherine of Siena, Catherine of Genoa, Bridget of Sweden, Christina the Astonishing, Margaret of Oingt. Like other women mystics, she was at times weakened by illness which she used for a closer walk with God in Christ in his passion:

Sometimes, notwithstanding that the said creature had a bodily sickness, the Passion of our merciful Lord Christ Jesus still so worked in her soul that at that time she did not feel her own illness, but wept and sobbed at the memory of our Lord's Passion, as though she saw him with her bodily eye suffering pain and Passion before her. Afterwards, when eight years were passed, her sickness abated, so that it did not come week by week as it did before, but then her cries and weeping increased so much that priests did not dare to give her communion openly in the church, but privately, in the Prior's chapel at Lynn, out of people's hearing. And in that chapel she had such high contemplation and so much confabulation with our Lord, inasmuch as she was put out of church for his love, for she cried at the time when she should receive communion as if her soul and her body were going to be parted, so that two men held her in their arms till her crying ceased, for she could not bear the abundance of love that she felt for the precious sacrament, which she steadfastly believed was very God and man in the form of bread. Then our blessed Lord said to her mind, 'Daughter, I will not have my grace hidden that I give you, for the busier people are to hinder it and prevent it, the more I shall spread it abroad and make it known to all the world.'[18]

After an agreed separation between her and her family, Margery travelled – Palestine, Assisi, Rome, Compostela,

Norway, Aachen, Danzig – and she travelled alone though among other pilgrims. One of her visits was to Norwich because she had heard of and perhaps had known someone who had read the works of the anchoress, Julian of Norwich;

> She told her about the grace God had put into her soul, of compunction, contrition, sweetness and devotion compassion with holy meditation and high contemplation and very many speeches and converse that our Lord spoke to her soul and also many wonderful revelations which she described to the anchoress to find out if there were any deception in them for the anchoress was expert in such things and could give good advice.[19]

Margery was not interested in Julian and even if she had heard of the record of Julian's revelations of the love of God she made no comment on them, nor does she record any personal details about Julian; instead, she records Julian as listening with courtesy and recommending obedience, charity and above all patience; perhaps one need say no more about the contrast between this emotional, affective, talkative woman, and the silence and wisdom of Julian.

The new feasts of the times reflect closely the spirituality of Margery: the Feast of the Passion (1334); the Five Wounds (1239); the Crown of Thorns (1230); the Compassion of the Virgin, and of the Precious Blood (1423). She is in so many ways a type of the middle-aged, middle-class housewife of the times and also of the individual whose enthusiasm bordered on hysteria for love of the person of Jesus: she was mistaken for a Lollard and arrested and tried in the aftermath of Sir John Oldcastle's rebellion. For her the way from the gulf of sorrow to the tower of truth lay firmly among the field full of folk.

Julian of Norwich 1342–1413

A contemporary of Geoffrey Chaucer (1340–1402) Julian wrote two books, one a long version of the other, called *Revelations of Divine Love*, expressing the flowering of English prose as well as containing the first sustained theology to be written in English. She lived as an anchoress in a cell built on to the wall of the church of St Julian in Norwich. In this century she has become well known and indeed popular but she was very little known in her own times and all but lost sight of in England at the Reformation. Her works were recovered and edited only at the end of the nineteenth century. There is only one manuscript of her first book, and that is contemporary with her; there are three of her second, but these are seventeenth- and eighteenth-century copies, all differing in details.

Like the English writers already discussed, Julian was of English middle-class birth, independent, outside structures of monastic life, and writing important works in the vernacular. She stands out from them, however, in that she was also a very great theologian writing real theology about the nature of love as it is in God. While most spiritual writers are helping the reader to love God and respond to that love, or recording personal experiences in a struggle with words to express the inexpressible, Julian quietly took the basic concept of the love that is God and explored it with ascetic thoroughness.

Julian was probably married, a widow who had lost one or more children in the plague. Thereafter she lived at home with her mother; she says that when she was 31 or 32 years old in 1373 she became very ill and thought she would die; a crucifix was held in front of her and it seemed to her to come alive and she saw through it the significance of the passion of Christ in vivid detail as the key to her own questioning of the relationship between love and suffering. She wrote her reflections down or more probably dictated them when she recovered. At some point thereafter she began to live as an anchoress. After thinking and meditating for 20 years, she wrote another longer version, both books being known under the title *Revelations of Divine Love*.

Unlike Margery Kempe, Julian was quite clear that to see visions was entirely neutral: 'because of the shewing I am not good but only if I love God the better.'[20] Like the *Cloud* author and Hilton she regarded Rolle's affective mysticism with suspicion and reserve. Like all the others, her understanding of the love of God underlies all her ideas: 'Love was our Lord's meaning.' The love of God within the Trinity is the basic pattern for her of thought and of life but this was no simple and easy discovery; on the contrary, her awareness of sin, death, sorrow and guilt made her ask a basic question: if God is all loving and redeeming, how does he see sin and pain and grief? Julian persistently asked this question about suffering, and especially about the greatest suffering of all which is that alienation from God called sin. Shown only love in God, she was acutely aware of sin and sorrow and evil and blame. She would not accept any easy answer, none which did not really take into account the fullness of love and the gravity of sin. 'I was not shown sin' she says and yet 'sin is the sharpest scourge'. The tower of love and truth was to be sought within the gulf of sorrow and the folk, for Julian, not outside but within the tower of truth: 'There are so many deeds which in our eyes are evilly done and lead to such great harms that it seems impossible to us that any good result should ever come from them.'[21]

And yet she believed that good is the end, not evil. The image that most helped her to clarify this was a parable of a Lord and Servant.

In the servant is comprehended the second person of the Trinity, and in the servant is comprehended Adam, that is to say all men. And therefore when I say 'the Son', that means the divinity which is equal to the Father, and when I say 'the servant', that means Christ's humanity, which is the true Adam. By the closeness of the servant is understood the Son, and by his standing to the left is understood Adam. The lord is God the Father, the servant is the Son, Jesus Christ, the Holy Spirit is the equal love which is in them both. When Adam fell, God's Son fell; because of the true union which was made in heaven, God's Son could not be separated from Adam, for by Adam I understand all mankind. Adam fell from death to life into the valley of this wretched world, and after that into hell. God's Son fell with Adam, into the valley of the womb of the maiden who was the first daughter of Adam, and that was to excuse Adam from blame in heaven and on earth; and powerfully he brought him out of hell. By the wisdom and the goodness which were in the servant is understood God's Son, by the labourer's poor clothing and the standing close by the left side, is understood Adam's humanity with all the harm and weakness which follow. For in all this our good Lord showed his own Son and Adam as only one man. The strength and the goodness that we have is from Christ Jesus, the weakness and blindness that we have is from Adam, which two were shown in the servant.[22]

This exposition of the doctrine of redemption is a true theology, concerned with the nature of God outside time and the one moment which is both creation and re-creation. God the Father creates man through his Son, who is the first Adam and redeems him in the same Son, the second Adam, and is ready to include Adam in the Trinity as he is alive in Christ by the Spirit. The moment of creation, redemption, sanctification are all one moment and the end is joy and confident trust: 'we are His crown, his blessed wife, the fair maiden of endless joy.'

With an unusual image for the Christian spiritual tradition, Julian also describes the love Christ has for us in terms of a mother, who suffers in bearing her children and gives her life in love for them, nurturing and caring for and receiving them back. This is an image first popularized by Anselm of Canterbury in his 'Prayer to Saint Paul' in his *Prayers and Meditations*, but given a new depth by Julian.

Given her picture of the all-embracing love of God, she writes for all, for 'mine even Christians', without excluding anyone from that category; 'all that shall be saved is Jesus and Jesus is all that shall be saved'. The way of redemption is for all the folk, not for an exclusive or esoteric group:

> I saw and understood that we may not in this life keep us from sin as completely as we shall in heaven . . . and we go at once to God in love. Neither on the one hand should we fall low in despair, nor on the other be over reckless as if we did not care but we should simply acknowledge that we may not stand for the twinkling of an eye except by the grace of God and we should reverently cleave to God in him only trusting.[23]

Her understanding of the cross, the centre and focus of all her thought, is again very unlike the self-blame of Margery Kempe or the emotional sweetness of Rolle or even general devotion in her own time. Her much quoted but misunderstood phrase 'All shall be well' was not an expression of easy confidence but integral to her understanding of the redemption:

Then our good Lord put a question to me: Are you well satisfied that I suffered for you? I said: Yes, good Lord, all my thanks to you; yes, good Lord, blessed may you be. Then Jesus our good Lord said: If you are satisfied, I am satisfied. It is a joy, a bliss, an endless delight to me that ever I suffered my Passion for you; and if I could suffer more, I should suffer more. We are His bliss, we are His reward. We are his crown.[24]

Conclusion

The message of the English mystics is certainly not one of ease and comfortableness, but of hope and love. Only after wrestling with God, like Jacob in the dark, and being like him permanently wounded, can anyone go towards the brother one has hated and say 'I see your face as the face of God'. They all used their own language, starting where they were, to express the gospel for the first time in English, with a theology of self-knowledge and God-knowledge, by submission and repentance exploring the reality of God. They spoke out of lives of independence and solitude, lived within a world torn and agonizing and filled with doubt. Between the tower of truth and the gulf of sorrow they stood within the field of folk and found it good. T. S. Eliot drew on the words of both *The Cloud of Unknowing* and the *Revelations of Divine Love* to express at the end of *Four Quartets* the hope which runs through them all:

> With the drawing of this Love and the voice of this Calling
> . . .
> A condition of complete simplicity
> (Costing not less than everything)
> And all shall be well and
> All manner of thing shall be well
> When the tongues of flame are infolded
> Into the crowned knot of fire
> And the fire and the rose are one.[25]

Notes

1. Philip de Mézières, *Letter to Richard II*, ed. G. W. Coopland (Liverpool: Liverpool University Press, 1975), p. 20.
2. Richard Rolle, *The Fire of Love*, tr. F. M. Compar (London: 1914) II, xii, p. 190.
3. Richard Rolle, *The Form of Living*, in *The English Writings of Richard Rolle*, ed. Rosemary Allen (Classics of Western Spirituality; London: SPCK, 1989), ch. 8, p. 171.
4. Rolle, *The Form of Living*, pp. 152–84.
5. *The Life and Lyrics of Richard Rolle*, tr. Francis Cooper (London: Dent, 1933), p. 269.
6. Walter Hilton, *The Scale of Perfection*, tr. Evelyn Underhill (London: Methuen, 1923), Bk I, ch. 92, p. 221.
7. Ibid., ch. 31, pp. 363–4.
8. Ibid., ch. 93, pp. 222–3.
9. *Cloud of Unknowing*, ed. James Walsh (London: SPCK, 1981), ch. V, p. 128.
10. *The Cloud of Unknowing with The Epistle of Privy Council*, tr. Justin McCann (London: Burns & Oates, 1924), *Epistle*, ch. VII, p. 124.
11. Ibid., *Cloud*, ch. XLVIII, p. 67.
12. Ibid., *Cloud*, ch. XXXII, p. 48.
13. *An Assessment of Inward Stirrings*, tr. James Walsh, in *The Pursuit of Wisdom* (New York: Paulist Press, 1988), p. 140.
14. *Epistle*, tr. McCann, ch. II, p. 108.
15. *Cloud*, tr. McCann, ch. LXXV, p. 101.
16. *The Book of Margery Kempe*, tr. B. A. Windeatt (Harmondsworth: Penguin, 1985), ch. 3, p. 48.
17. Ibid., ch. 56, p. 177.
18. Ibid.
19. Ibid., ch. 18, pp. 77–8.
20. Julian of Norwich, *Showings*, tr. James Walsh (London: SPCK, 1978), ch. 9, p. 191.
21. Ibid., ch. 32, p. 232.
22. Ibid., ch. 51, pp. 274–5.
23. Ibid., ch. 52, p. 281.
24. Ibid., ch. 12 p. 144.
25. T. S. Eliot, 'Little Gidding', *Collected Poems 1909–1962* (London: Faber & Faber, 1963), pp. 222–3.

5

THE SPANISH MYSTICS

COLIN THOMPSON

It is generally agreed that St Teresa of Ávila (1515–82) and St John of the Cross (1542–91) stand at the summit of what, rightly or wrongly, we have come to call the Western mystical tradition. Teresa recruited the young John at a point of crisis in his own journey, when he had dropped out of university after completing just one year of his theology degree at Salamanca (having survived three years of arts) and was on the verge of abandoning his Order for the Carthusians because they lived a stricter, more enclosed and prayerful life than the one he had found among the Carmelites. She persuaded him to begin among male members of the Order the reform she had already initiated among the sisters. It was a move which would bring both of them, but John especially, suffering and opprobrium. For some five years, between 1572 and 1577, John was confessor to the nuns at the Convent of the Incarnation in Ávila, while Teresa was Prioress. That was the time of their closest association, the seedbed, perhaps, for that Spanish Carmelite contribution to the history of Western spirituality which has proved to be so decisive in its formation. They are remarkably like and unlike each other. Rather than attempting to reconcile them where they appear to differ, I prefer to see them as complementary; and at risk of over-simplification, I would look for that complementarity in the dialogue between Teresa's relative muddle about structuring the life of prayer, her rootedness and her humanity, and John of the Cross's relative clarity and systematic approach, his sense of the divine otherness and the ways in which he pursues the principles he enunciates to their logical and theological conclusion (I am thinking of his prose writings here; his poetry is another matter altogether).

The story I have to tell is of one and the same journey, undertaken by two people and described in their writings, but from very different perspectives. The journey begins with self-knowledge and introspection, the search for communion with the living God within the human soul, and it ends with union with God and transformation in him. On the way there are many obstacles to be tackled and pitfalls to be recognized and avoided. Teresa's writings themselves mirror this process and often provide a vivid first-hand account of the confusion and distress she suffered, as well as of the experiences of God's love which brought her joy and confidence, especially at moments of great crisis. Her *Life*, as Rowan Williams points out, represents 'one specific moment in Teresa's development – her first attempt at a coherent overview of what had happened and was still happening to her'.[1] Although in it she is searching for a coherent narrative out of the story of her life to that point, and using well-known and authoritative writings to guide her, such as Augustine's *Confessions* and hagiographical literature, there are many aspects of prayer which remain unclear to her, and her inner trajectory still has a distance to go. Her *Way of Perfection* and the *Book of Foundations* represent an advance, but it is only with *The Interior Castle* that we reach a mature and assured statement of her account of mystical prayer. Her writing, therefore, is progressive, and one should not look for absolute consistency between the parts. It is rooted not only in her own life of prayer but also, essentially, in the life of the first Discalced Carmelite communities, as the *Way* and the *Foundations* demonstrate.

The journey as mirrored in the writings of John of the Cross reads differently. That is because he writes from the perspective of the end of the journey, looking back over its course. In doing so, he is both much less personal and far more analytical than Teresa. His journey, though, has its own tension and ambiguity. Its first witness is a small number of poems which, as literary artefacts, are regarded as among the highest achievements of the Golden Age of Spain, a period of great cultural brilliance, which roughly occupies the sixteenth and seventeenth centuries. These poems are sensuous, ardent, lyrical, intensely beautiful, mysterious. They use the language of human love. But the second witness to his journey is the series of commentaries he wrote on these verses – *The Ascent of Mount Carmel* and *The Dark Night of the Soul*, effectively one treatise, purporting to expound his poem beginning 'On a dark night';

his *Spiritual Canticle* explains his longest poem, of that name; and the *Living Flame of Love* the third of his greatest poems. The *Ascent* and the *Dark Night* are unfinished; the *Spiritual Canticle* and the *Flame* continued to be revised, and their problematic manuscript and textual histories have occupied the critics for most of this century. Teresa too was a reviser: to the first version of her *Life* (1561–2) she added chapters 11–22, the famous treatise on the four waters of prayer, and chapters 32–40, which, among other things, recount the history of her first foundation, the Convent of San José, in Ávila.

Where do mystics come from? One answer is that they are called by divine grace. Another, and not necessarily in opposition to it, is that the way has been prepared for them. The first three decades of the sixteenth century in Spain were a time of great religious turmoil, and many of the issues raised but not always resolved then find an echo in the great decades of devotional and mystical writing, the 1560s, 70s and 80s, when not only Teresa and John were active but other writers, much more popular at the time, like the Dominican Fray Luis de Granada and the Augustinians Fray Luis de León and Malón de Chaide were publishing their works in the vernacular.

I cannot in the space available do more than sketch in the historical and intellectual background which helps us to understand the contribution of Teresa and John to a spiritual tradition long in the making, and I shall therefore concentrate on Spain, rather than the history of apophatic theology or medieval mystical traditions. Spain remains one of the unknown lands of Europe. Our image has been formed by the promoters of tourism: bullfights, flamenco, hot sunshine, a carefree life on the beach. This has little to do with the real Spain, the second most mountainous country in Europe, a country of great extremes of climate, flora and fauna, and of different peoples and languages. The warm, wet north-west and the sub-tropical south are as different as Ireland is from North Africa. In the sixteenth century, Spain ruled over the largest empire the world had ever seen. The union of the crowns of Castile and Aragón under Ferdinand and Isabella, the Catholic Monarchs, had made Spain into a nation-state, and the final surrender of the last bastion of Islamic rule in the peninsula, when the Catholic monarchs took triumphant possession of the

Kingdom of Granada in 1492, united the nation under a single faith. Those Jews who refused to convert to Christianity were expelled that same year and scattered across North Africa, the Balkans and the Middle East in what came to be known as Sephardic communities. The continuing presence in Spain of large numbers of people descended from *conversos*, or converted Jews, as of *moriscos*, the remnant Moorish population, caused the State and the Church serious problems, and is at the heart of that lamentable distinction between old Christians and new Christians, between those who could prove that their descent had been untainted by any Jewish or Moorish blood and those, like Teresa herself, who could not.

During the closing decades of the fifteenth century, Ferdinand and Isabella actively promoted the reform of the religious orders in their kingdoms. Their motives were partly or mostly political, but one of the results was an increase in devotional reading in monastic circles. The process of reform was overseen by Cardinal Cisneros de Ximénez, Primate of Spain from 1495, and after the death of Philip of Burgundy, heir to Ferdinand, in 1506, briefly Regent of Spain. One of his descendants on a brother's side would, by one of those nice historical ironies, move to England in the eighteenth century and marry into the family of Oliver Cromwell. Cisneros himself also encouraged scholarship, notably in the founding of the Trilingual College at Alcalá, near Madrid, where his great Complutensian Polyglot Bible, finished in 1517, was prepared. The Benedictine Abbot of Monserrat, one of the most ancient and influential of all religious houses in the peninsula, was García de Cisneros, a cousin of the Cardinal-Archbishop, who both wrote and had translated into the vernacular a steady stream of medieval devotional and mystical works, and printed the first such works written directly in the vernacular. His own *Exercitatorio de la vida spiritual* (*Book of Exercises for the Spiritual Life*) of 1500 was, as Terence O'Reilly has pointed out, the first manual of methodical prayer to be published in Castilian, though it drew heavily on writings in the tradition of the *devotio moderna*, as well as by St Bonaventure and by Carthusian authors.[2] This tradition of vernacular works offering a method for progress in meditative and contemplative prayer was to grow through the first half of the sixteenth century in Spain. It is surely not fanciful to regard, as critics like Melquiades Andrés do, this confluence of currents of reform and observantism with the rise of a vernacular literature of affective spirituality as the seed-bed from which the glories of Carmelite mysticism would grow.

But while reform of the religious orders would continue under Philip II, especially among those orders which had remained unreformed, the Mercedarians, Trinitarians and Carmelites, the possibilities of reading vernacular works on prayer were to be rudely interrupted by the first Inquisitorial Index of 1559, which banned large numbers of them, including some which had most helped Teresa, as she herself records in her *Life* (26.6).[3] Teresa had been brought up in an atmosphere of reading good books, that is, once she had overcome her addiction to pulp fiction, in the shape of chivalric romances, which, she tells us, she read by day and night, though hidden from her father. Happily, such reading, frowned upon by humanists and churchmen alike, did not addle her brains, as it did Don Quixote's. Both her father and her uncle were avid readers of the new generation of spiritual works: one begins to sense just how quickly the invention of printing developed and a reading public grew. Among the books which helped her were Francisco de Osuna's *Tercer abecedario* (*Third Spiritual Alphabet*), with its teaching on *recogimiento*, withdrawal, recollection; a translation of St Gregory's *Moralia*, which helped her to view her own trials and tribulations in a positive way, as a means of serving God; the Franciscan Alonso de Madrid's *Arte de servir a Dios* (*Art of Serving God*), with its emphasis on the humanity of Christ and on mental prayer; and Bernardino de Laredo's *Subida del monte Sión* (*Ascent of Mount Zion*), which describes the union of the soul with God, and which caught her attention for its teaching on the state of *no pensar nada*, 'not thinking of anything', during prayer. She marked her copy and this is still treasured as a relic by the nuns of San José today.[4] On the other hand, she complained that many spiritual works were much better at describing than explaining different states of prayer, which was little use to beginners.[5] She also read 'El Cartujano', Ludolph of Saxony's immensely popular *Vita Christi*, translated into Spanish by order of Cardinal Cisneros in 1502.[6] But if there is one work more than any other which

69

gives her *Life* its shape and flavour it is Augustine's *Confessions*. Significantly, she comments that when she read it she seemed to see herself in it.[7] In Augustine she found someone who had bared his soul with total honesty, a figure of indisputable authority; and though her story of youthful flirtations and love of fine clothes and make-up, as well as of escapist literature, is hardly his struggle with sexuality and the competing philosophies of the fourth-century Roman Empire, Teresa was profoundly affected by it. In many ways the style and structure of the *Life* is modelled on the *Confessions*, with their characteristic mixture of narrative, introspective analysis, prayers of penitence and outbursts of praise. The early struggles of Teresa, recorded in her *Life*, need to be understood against the contemporary background of controversy about mental prayer, and especially about the role of women as its practitioners.

The first three decades of the sixteenth century in Spain were marked by an openness to new ideas, especially the influence of Renaissance humanism. In particular, the works of Erasmus, translated into Spanish, enjoyed a huge popularity, with their attacks on decadent scholasticism and monasticism and their ideal of the *philosophia Christi*, which was open to all believers, however simple. The call of Erasmus to an inward grasp of the truths represented in ritual and image struck a responsive chord in many parts of Europe, but perhaps most of all in Spain. For some time it was a chord which sounded in harmony with earlier writing, like the immensely influential *Contemptus mundi*, known to us as *The Imitation of Christ*, and ascribed to Thomas à Kempis, as well as the new vernacular works to which I have alluded. The spread of the Lutheran Reform put an end to that, for the Spanish king, Charles V, was also the ruler of the Netherlands and nominally of the Holy Roman Empire, the German States. For that and other reasons a markedly more conservative atmosphere came to dominate Spanish religious life, and though there was a greater pluralism in theological thinking than is generally realized in the second half of the century, this has come to be associated with the triumph of post-Tridentine Catholicism and the ruthless suppression of any strand of opinion deemed incompatible with it.

The reform of the monastic orders had played its part in the call of members to a deeper life of prayer, particularly by recalling them back to their primitive Rule, exactly the pattern which was to inspire Teresa and John in their fiercely-resisted reform of the Carmel. But the scandals associated with the so-called *alumbrados*, or *illuminati* (the enlightened ones) created a climate of suspicion, especially in relation to women, who were often at the centre of these groups of people who met regularly for prayer and teaching. The first arrests of *alumbrados* took place in 1524, and were followed by an Edict of Faith defining and condemning their doctrine. Much of what is known about these groups comes from the records of the Inquisition, which are one-sided, to say the least: in his recent study of the *alumbrados* (1992) Alastair Hamilton describes the 48 propositions in the edict as 'mainly statements or snatches of conversation overheard by hostile witnesses.'[8] One of them, significantly, was that 'prayer must be mental and not vocal'.[9] There can be little doubt that the *alumbrado* phenomenon through the sixteenth century was more varied and complex than its attackers believed: the first groups seem to have followed a form of evangelical pietism not far removed from the *devotio moderna* or Erasmian spirituality, while later groups were more clearly influenced by Lutheranism, or characterized by sexual laxity, quietism and antinomianism. But in a sense that does not matter for our story. What concerns us is the fear on the part of a woman like Teresa that the experiences she had begun to have might prove delusory, or at worst, heretical and diabolical. Just as she had no idea what Lutheranism was, though she mentions it with horror from time to time, so too it was enough to whisper the word *alumbrado* to set suspicious tongues wagging and Inquisitorial noses sniffing. The conservative view held that nuns should content themselves with vocal prayer: with the Choir Office and with those prayers like the *Pater noster*, which the Church prescribed for regular use. If they limited themselves to these, they would run no risk of delusion or deception. Once they were encouraged to pray in their minds and in their own words and through their own images, who could say where that might lead? For women, even those who had been educated, were theologically illiterate (hence Teresa's frequent references, especially in her earlier writings, to *letrados*, the learned churchmen who sometimes were able to help her understand, but at other times were, she thinks, at least as ignorant of prayer as she was). Teresa's story is in many ways one of the vindication of a more far-reaching spirituality for women than the Church had generally tolerated, and it is notable that her first editor, the great Augustinian writer and scholar, Fray Luis de León, and the influential though more cautious Dominican, Domingo Báñez, both in their different ways recognize that her gifts and her teaching are divinely inspired. One should not underestimate that, in the context of the age, a woman, with a *converso* background, denounced from time to time to the Inquisition, comes to be regarded as an authority in teaching the way to union with God in contemplative prayer and is canonized, long before St John of the Cross, for example, received similar recognition. Teresa herself was quite capable of subverting her critics: she devotes the second half of her *Way of Perfection* (chapters 43–72) to an exposition of the vocal prayer *par excellence*, the Our Father, but teaches her nuns to use it as the basis for mental prayer.

To conclude this brief background survey, I should only add a word of caution about *conversos* and about the Inquisition. It is as easy to look for explanations for Teresa's attitudes, say, to honour and social status, in the fact that one of her grandparents was a *converso* as it is to attribute all kinds of features of the age to the sinister presence of the Inquisition. I do not wish to deny that either have their place. But it is too facile to appeal to them as simple explanations. Many distinguished Spaniards of the period were descended from *conversos*, and they do not all exhibit the same attitudes. Our impression of the Inquisition owes more to the Black Legend, created by Spanish liberals and American and German Quakers and Protestants in the early nineteenth century, and given fictional form by Edgar Allan Poe in *The Pit and the Pendulum*, than it does to historical accuracy. All countries had mechanisms of State repression. The Spanish Inquisition was probably no worse, and in some cases was better, than these. Its major fault was its slowness and bureaucracy, not its use of torture, which was limited. Teresa's brushes with it, for example, were relatively trivial and easily dismissed. But her first editor, Luis de León, spent nearly five years in the cells of the Inquisition in Valladolid, while the case against him and two colleagues from Salamanca proceeded with agonizing slowness. He was vindicated, but one of his colleagues died in prison before the case was completed. That is a more representative picture, though *autos-da-fe* certainly happened from time to time.

Teresa's maturest work on prayer is her *Moradas del castillo interior*, or *Interior Castle*, written in 1577. Many of her earlier struggles have been resolved: no one now seriously believes her to be possessed by the devil, or sick and deluded. Her dream of reforming her Order through a return to the poverty, enclosure and prayer which had marked its foundations has begun to be realized at San José. On the other hand, the work was finished less than a week before the Carmelite Reform was thrown into convulsion by the kidnapping and imprisonment of John of the Cross. Relatively little is new in the first four mansions, though her presentation is more orderly, and the image itself is striking. What I find telling is her own sense of progress. When she comes to describe the difference between two ways in which water reaches a fountain and fills it, one over many aqueducts and with much effort, and the other directly and silently from the source,[10] she is making a simpler and less laboured distinction than she does in chapters 11–22 of the *Life*, where prayer is likened to four ways of watering, of progressively diminishing human effort, without losing the essential point: the movement from the mind's active construction of words and images to the mind's being grasped by God and held by him. She goes on to say: 'Maybe in these inner things I am contradicting what I have written elsewhere, but that shouldn't surprise anyone, because in the almost fifteen years that have gone by since I wrote before, the Lord has perhaps granted me greater clarity in these matters than I then had.'[11]

She is now able to trace the transition from the Prayer of Quiet to union, and from the spiritual betrothal to the spiritual marriage. When she writes of the secret union which takes place in the innermost centre of the soul,[12] she is probably reflecting what she had learnt in her many discussions with John of the Cross. But she is insistent, as she had been in the *Life*, that however high the soul progresses, it should never abandon meditation on the humanity of Christ. In this respect her

73

teaching differs sharply from St John's, and I do not think that the two can be reconciled in this regard, or that it matters. Teresa always feels more grounded than John, always sounds more insistent that however lofty the soul's experience of God may be, it must never lose touch with the real world. Nowhere is this clearer than at the end of the *Interior Castle*: 'This is what prayer is for, daughters; this is what the spiritual marriage is for, so that works may always be the result, works';[13] and, taking the traditional distinction between Martha as the type of the active life and Mary of the contemplative: 'Believe me, Martha and Mary must always go together to receive the Lord and have him ever with them'.[14] 'If you fail to seek and practise virtues, you will always be dwarves.'[15]

One of the things I find encouraging about Teresa is that her teaching on prayer was the result of uncertainty, struggle, conflict and suffering. She does not write about St John's dark night of the soul as such, but it is clear from her account of the years of pain she experienced, not knowing whether God or the devil was inspiring her, that her authority as a teacher was won out of wrestling with difficulties. Many of the problems modern readers experience in finding their way through St John's commentaries are connected both with the process of their composition and the audience to which they were directed. As Eulogio Pacho has pointed out in the prologue to his 1982 edition of St John's *Complete Works*, the main lines of the argument, especially in the *Ascent*, quickly become muddied 'in a tangle of themes and schemes of increasing complexity and detail'.[16] It is easy to lose the overall orientation of the work in these excurses, which may themselves be the result of an often-interrupted process of composition in the first place and of hurried revisions in the second. St John addressed himself to a very limited readership, not to the general public – to a small number of friars and nuns of the Discalced Carmelite Order who had advanced far on the road and who needed better guidance than they were able to find from any available spiritual treatises or from their confessors. They lived in a monastic environment in which ascetic and penitential practices were taken for granted, and St John might well have believed that outside such a context it was impossible to understand his teaching, or, worse still, that it would prove misleading. He wrote three or four treatises, depending on how the relationship between the *Ascent of Mount Carmel* and the *Dark Night of the Soul* is viewed. Each is cast in the form of a commentary on one of his poems, though the *Ascent* and the *Night* pay less attention to this than do the *Spiritual Canticle* and the *Living Flame of Love*. The genre of these works is difficult to fix. They are part poetic gloss, part biblical commentary, part ascetic and moral treatise, part devotional text, with numerous digressions; but the balance between these elements is a shifting one. Historically, the *Canticle* came first, in the sense that by 1579 St John had begun to write commentaries on individual verses of the poem at the request of nuns who found his poems beautiful but beyond their comprehension. The *Ascent* and the *Night* were written at different times during the early 1580s but develop the same fundamental teaching, based on the image of the dark night of the soul as expounded in four different phases.

The structure of the *Canticle* and the *Flame* is relatively straightforward. The *Canticle* is patterned according to the three traditional ways of the mystical journey, the purgative way of beginners (C 1–5), the illuminative way of proficients (CB 6–13; CA 6–12) and the unitive way of the perfect (CB 14–40; CA 13–39). The spiritual betrothal (CB 13; CA 12) and the spiritual marriage (CB 22; CA 27) fall within these stages. This is not explained until the commentary is well advanced (CB 22.3; CA 27.3). The *Flame* has greater unity, with the important exception of the long digression on spiritual direction.[17]

The *Ascent-Night* is another story. S 1 begins with a complex piece of biblical exegesis which divides the night into three parts, at once setting up a counterpoint its overall fourfold scheme. It then defines the division between sense and spirit and analyses two kinds of damage caused by the sensual appetites of the soul, which are described in a series of five verbs, the exposition of which covers the central chapters (6–10). S 2–3 explain the active night of the spirit as this affects the three faculties in turn, the intellect (S 2), the memory (S 3.1–15) and the will (S 3.16–45), to which the three theological virtues of faith, hope and love correspond. Thus two further triple perspectives are introduced, which control the exposition. N 1 begins with a series of chapters patterned on the seven deadly spiritual sins (1–7), which St John himself admits are really out of place (1.1), while towards the end of N 2 a miniature treatise on the ten steps of the mystical ladder of divine love interrupts the exposition of the passive night of the spirit, prompted by St John's arrival at the second line of the second verse of the poem, with its image of the 'secret ladder'.

The beginning of the *Ascent* is a good illustration of the difficulties readers face. Having established the sense–spirit polarity, St John explains why this moment of transition is called night.[18] His account shows how complex the structure of his argument can be, but it is sufficiently brief (only 50 lines of text in the BAC edition[19]) for it not to be too daunting. He gives three reasons, each threefold in form. First, it is called night because of its point of origin: the soul must abandon her pleasure in worldly things, and this negation is night to the senses. It is also night because of the road which must be followed, faith, which is dark as night to the intellect. It is night too by virtue of its goal, God himself, who is a dark night to the soul in this life. His symbol therefore represents the whole enterprise, in both its human and divine aspects; it is an all-embracing symbol, comprehensive, multivalent, and only context can determine which particular meaning of the three is intended.

Second, he proceeds, as he had promised, to find scriptural confirmation for his argument, to demonstrate that his doctrine of the dark night is not his own invention but the authoritative word of Scripture. His exegesis strikes the modern reader as fanciful and improbable, but it follows the normal methods of the age. St John is almost invariably scrupulous in establishing a direct verbal connection between his teaching and Scripture, and he regards the Bible as source of his authority, in that it confirms at every stage his teaching. In the Book of Tobit, young Tobias is commanded by the angel who accompanies him on his journey to spend three nights alone before he may marry his bride, whose first six husbands have all unfortunately been killed by the Devil on the night of their honeymoon. In the first night he is told that he must 'burn the fish's heart',[20] and it is this reference to the heart and its burning which prompts the exegetical connection, since the human heart is to burn all her other affections in the fire of divine love. In the second night Tobias is to be admitted 'into the company of the holy patriarchs',[21] which is faith, since they are the fathers of faith. In the third, he will receive 'the blessing',[22] which is the union of Bride and Beloved. He will be joined to his wife 'in the fear of the Lord', since such fear, when perfect, transforms the soul in love (an unstated but implicit reference to 1 John 4.18, 'perfect love casteth out fear'). For modern readers, this is a very obscure passage on which to hang the whole doctrine of the dark night. But for St John and his contemporaries all Scripture, when rightly interpreted, possessed the same authority. More importantly, by making the association with Tobit, he introduces images which are central to his endeavour: the journey beset by tribulations, the curing of blindness, and the celebration of marriage.

Third, he tells us that 'these three parts of the night together form one night',[23] as natural night does. The divisions only exist as parts of a whole. As darkness falls, things recede; at midnight faith walks in the deepest darkness; as daybreak approaches, God's presence is about to dawn. Having established the symbol as scriptural, St John now illustrates it from nature. The pattern is an important one, repeated in the many analogies he will draw from nature and art in support of his argument. Experience, revelation and reason all have their part to play in this ascent of the mountain which is also a journey through the long night. The experience needs to be placed in the context of biblical faith before it can be correctly interpreted, but nature and reason have their part to play in the creation and exploration of the symbol, the only form of language able to unite and transcend these separate realms.

St John's teaching rests on a number of fundamental principles which need to be grasped before the particular details of his argument can become clear. They are characteristically woven into the dense texture of his writing, and need to be picked out, so that the complex patterns of discourse he creates do not overwhelm the larger design. His most famous creation, the often-quoted 'dark night of the soul', is endowed in his thought with a precision and a scope which is evident from the outset and which belies its much looser contemporary usage. Before any assessment of the significance of his teaching can be attempted, these broad principles must be established, since they govern his analysis of the human self and its quest for fulfilment. They are not always self-evident at first reading: St John's prologue to the *Ascent* says as much, with its acknowledgment that readers may find the work somewhat obscure and benefit from a second reading.

St John's subject is the human search for God (the active part of the dark night) and the divine search for humanity (the passive). To undertake this, he makes an analysis of the human personality, its constitution, its conflicts and its potential. This analysis finds its fullest and most systematic expression in the *Ascent-Night*, but it is present in the other commentaries too. He divides his famous symbol into the night of the senses and the night of the spirit, each of which presents a double aspect of activity and passivity. The commentary follows this fourfold structure: the active night of the senses (S 1), the active night of the spirit (S 2–3), the passive night of the senses (N 1) and the passive night of the spirit (N 2). The two nights of the senses occupy relatively little space, since they relate to ascetic principles and practices familiar to his monastic audience. But the active and passive nights of the spirit are treated at much greater length, despite the fact that in both cases the commentary is unfinished. The reason for this disparity is that, as he says in the prologue to the *Canticle*, 'there are many things written for beginners',[24] that is, there is no shortage of material to guide people through the nights of the senses. But the night of the spirit, especially in its passive mode, is very little understood, and presents a much graver problem to spiritual directors, whose charges may well have advanced further on the journey than they have themselves. St John's originality as a spiritual theologian lies largely in the fact that he was the first writer ever to have undertaken so complete an analysis of the higher reaches of prayer. For this reason, his attacks on inexperienced spiritual directors in the prologue to the *Ascent* and what appears to be a lengthy and passionate digression on the same topic in the *Flame*,[25] form an integral part of his argument. It is the lack of appropriate written guidance for them and their charges which has prompted him to undertake his own account, so that souls are not handicapped in their progress. No doubt he is reflecting, among others, on Teresa's problems with those confessors who told her that her visions and raptures were demonic.

For his task, St John uses a technical vocabulary largely derived from his training in the arts and scholastic philosophy and theology. Some of his terminology is no longer in common use; other expressions have changed meaning. 'Substantial', for example (like 'essential') does not have the modern meaning of 'considerable' ('necessary') but the more philosophical 'pertaining to the substance (essence) of'. 'Accidental' does not mean 'by chance' but belongs to the originally Aristotelian distinction between the substance (true nature) and the accidents (outward appearance) of an object, without which, for example, the Catholic doctrine of transubstantiation is incomprehensible. His distinctions and definitions are often difficult for readers today, even the theologically educated, but happily, since few of the friars and none of the nuns for whom he was writing were, he provides many similes and examples in order to make his teaching accessible, though these are rarely as vivid or developed as Teresa's. They do not have the intellectual rigour of his analysis, but they support it and are important guides for the task of translation and interpretation.

Some of the medieval schematizations he uses – the seven deadly sins, the four cardinal virtues – are familiar, even if we cannot always name each one. Others, like the three theological virtues, are stranger, but these are simply the technical term for the 'three things which last for ever, faith, hope and love', expounded so nobly by St Paul in 1 Cor. 13. In St John's systems these virtues correspond to the three 'faculties' of the soul, understanding, memory and will, and play an essential part in their reordering towards God. Nowhere more than in his picture of how the human being works does the cultural gap between his world and ours interpose. None of his terminology, however, should mask the fact that St John is always thinking in terms of the whole person. Many articles and books have been written to clarify their significance, but such attempts tend to lose sight of any integrated picture of what human beings are and how they work. Equally, his divisions, subdivisions and digressions are there to make his analysis of the whole person more profound, far-reaching and inclusive.

St John's prime concern is the inner life of an individual.

When he uses the word *alma*, 'soul', he means the whole inner life of a person, not that part which according to many religions survives physical death. It therefore includes both the conscious and unconscious modes of operation of the self and a range of feelings and desires, many of them construed in negative terms, which would not generally now be associated with the concept of 'soul'.

The antithesis between sense and spirit, so strongly marked in his writing, should not be interpreted negatively, as denial of the body and exaltation of abstinence from all kinds of bodily desire. The *Ascent* opens with a number of statements which correct such misinterpretations. First, any disorder or imperfection in the human senses is the result of a disorder of the will: not the wrong information, but wrong choices. The senses in themselves are not the cause, but how the will chooses to use them. For that reason, not only human senses but also the human spirit requires purification.[26] Sin is a spiritual sickness, the root cause of symptoms which manifest themselves in the misuse of the senses. St John divides the soul into a 'sensitive' and a 'spiritual' part, and occasionally also refers to the centre of the soul. He does not regard these as entities or locations, but rather as modalities of the inner life which are easy to distinguish at their extremes and useful for the sake of analysis.

The soul is where the image and likeness of God is to be found, and therefore the proper place to look in order to find him. She is created expressly for the purpose of communing with him. But she is full of other kinds of knowledge and desire. St John, in accordance with his Aristotelian-Thomist training, regards knowledge of the outside world as mediated purely through the five senses: 'when God infuses the soul into the body, it is like a smooth, flat tablet on which nothing is painted, and apart from what it comes to know through the senses, nothing is communicated to it naturally from any other source'.[27] The 'sensitive' part of the soul represents that part of the inner life which is lived under the sway of sensual desires – when, for example, someone is overpowered by anger, lust or envy, or is greedy for worldly recognition or full of ambition. Such desires may well motivate those who seek the spiritual life: when, for example, they want others to believe that they are acting for the glory of God, whereas their true motives are self-centredness and the desire to impress others with a show of devotion or the favours God has granted. Religion itself, therefore, though spiritual in appearance, can easily become distorted into a manifestation of misplaced human desire. A great deal of the power and originality of St John's analysis of the dark night of the soul is found in the unmasking of religion of this kind, which speaks the language of serving God but which exalts the self above all else.

The 'spiritual' part of the soul represents that deeper, hidden mode of being of which we are not normally aware, but which is closer to its true nature and purpose. The aim of the ascetic life, with its works of mortification and self-denial, is to break the senses' stranglehold on motive, thought and action, so that the truly spiritual nature of the soul, governed by reason and enlightened by faith, can reassert its control. Plato's metaphor for the soul's imprisonment in the body was submarine, not terrestrial. The sea both erodes and deforms it, encrusting it with shells, seaweed and rocks, so that it can no longer be seen as it is (the sense, perhaps, of Shakespeare's image of 'sea-change' in *The Tempest*). This prison is therefore like an active, living organism to which fresh layers are constantly being added, with the result that it becomes correspondingly more difficult to imagine what it would be like free of such accretions or how it could act independently of them.

Whether or not St John was aware of the exact Platonic image, its sense remains basic to his thought. The soul is unable to act in conformity with its divine origin, because the deposits of repeated mistaken choices build up like accretions and the choices themselves become so habitual that they appear neutral or even good. People get used to thinking about themselves and their world in a particular way, which slips into becoming the only way they think. They remember particular pleasures and want to repeat them because they are gratifying. Ingrained habits of thought and desire lead them to make the same choices, over and over again, which accumulate to damage their capacity to respond to God or even lead them to feel that he is superfluous. It is not that the objects of our choice are bad in themselves. No created object can be, for all were created good in the mind and purpose of God. In the middle of a discussion of certain mystical states, St John slips in a principle which is of great importance for understanding the whole of his negative approach: that 'God does not destroy nature, but rather perfects it.'[28] He is not a Manichaean or any other kind of dualist, and it is an error to regard his teaching as a denial of creation or of the body, because if you follow the journey to its end, in the fourth book of the *Living Flame*, you reach his vision of creation transfigured. There, the whole creation, from its tiniest and frailest elements to all the constructs of human power and the heavenly realms themselves, move together in a single unity because, in St John's terms, creation is seen from the radically different perspective of God, rather than God being read through his works in creation. What he does is to unmask the damaging imperialism of the senses under which unredeemed humanity lives, largely unaware of its presence, in order to give priority to the spirit as the object of the mind's contemplation, the will's choices and the memory's contents. Only then will it be possible to see and to love without desiring to possess all those elements of our created lives which otherwise through our desire and possessiveness entrap us. So drastic a reversal of accustomed priorities cannot be achieved without a terrible struggle, but the conflict and pain are worthwhile because they open the way to the new humanity.

The soul's journey has both active and passive modes,[29] a distinction it is easy to misunderstand, and a misunderstanding which can end in a serious misreading of St John. The active includes everything human power can achieve to assist progress. The passive sounds like a state of inertia, which it is not. Put one way, it is the direct action of God on the soul and is a gift, not an achievement or reward for work done. It belongs as such to the wisdom and liberty of God, and is given according to his unfathomable purposes. Put another way, when the soul is passive, she is in a state of receptiveness. Her natural processes are stilled and her faculties are no longer occupied with particular images, concepts, memories or desires. Instead they experience a 'simple' or 'general' desire for God, the reduction of desire to its barest essentials, desire-in-itself for God-in-himself, rather than desire aroused, say, by an act of meditation on a moment from the life of Christ. The soul waits upon God with 'loving attention': that is her whole work and activity. If waiting brings only darkness and a keen sense of the absence of God, this must be borne patiently and faithfully, and must not affect the normal commitments of daily living. For through bearing the pain and suffering of these passive nights the soul is brought to greater knowledge of herself and of God.

Passivity, therefore, is neither a state of idleness nor that complete abandonment to the will of God which has traditionally been judged as heretical. When properly understood, it involves the letting go of everything which could hinder the work of God upon the soul and is, in reality, another form of activity: the activity of being receptive to something from without. In *Ascent* 2.15.2 St John likens it to having the eyes open and receiving light, which suggests that it is not a state of complete absence of human activity but of preparation to receive a gift. It is not hard to find other analogies. In order to become wholly engrossed in a play or a piece of music, the mind needs to be cleared of other, extraneous concerns. If it finds itself contemplating shopping lists, unanswered letters or the person in front, even if it is thinking devotional thoughts, it will not be free to concentrate on the spectacle or the sound. When it becomes free, it is not in a state of idleness, in which things float in and out of the mind with no particular purpose, but in a state of receptiveness which allows all its faculties to be wholly engaged in the act of watching or listening. It can be very difficult to move from everyday activity to this receptive mode. St John's active nights of sense and spirit, the ways in which the soul may habituate herself to emptying the faculties of all their other concerns, are intended to enable her to become receptive to what God will give her in the passive nights, gifts for which will there will be no room if she is busy with other concerns.

St John is easy to misrepresent. Two or three quotations taken out of context can create the impression of a man so obsessed by the dangers of any kind of material beauty that it had to be spurned. A reading of his three great poems in the *lira* metre should be enough to correct this, but their sensual images are rarely seen to be part of his theology. Yet a careful reading reveals that all St John's negations are made for the sake of a greater affirmation. The negative side of his teaching is therefore never an end in itself, but a means towards a more positive end. This can be traced back into the symbolism of the dark night itself. Divine light is experienced as darkness because of its blinding intensity, not because it actually is dark. In *Dark Night* 2.5 he tackles the paradox of how it is that divine light can be called darkness. His answer goes back to an Aristotelian principle: the brighter and clearer divine things are in themselves, the darker and more hidden they are to the soul. Thus, the brighter the light, the more the owl is blinded; and the more directly one looks at the sun, the more one is too.[30] That is why Dionysius and other mystical theologians call infused contemplation a 'ray of darkness'. It is painful for the soul to receive, because of her remaining imperfections, and she feels that God is against her and she against him.[31] The weight of it is such that sometimes she feels as if her whole being 'is suffering and in such agony under some huge, dark burden that she would think death a relief and a boon'.[32] Later, St John explains that the experience of darkness is soul-produced and not inherent in the light: 'the darkness ... is not darkness or evil produced by the light, but by the soul herself, and the light illumines her so that she can see it'.[33] The dark night seems to be as much about the soul's creatureliness as her sinfulness. Its sufferings are themselves part of the cure of sin and the preparation to receive divine light.[34]

St John's commentaries can also give the impression that the spiritual life is characterized by a series of recognizable steps along which the soul must pass: once the map is unfolded, all the features to be encountered on the way can be identified. Though there is some truth in this, it gives the impression of a system far more finished and fixed than is the case. There is a flexibility and a vitality about his teaching which is inherent in the very way he writes and which makes it a living organism rather than set in tablets of stone – more, in other words, like Teresa's accounts than at first sight appears. This can be seen in a number of ways: the unfinished nature of the treatises, the repetitions and digressions they contain, and the images of movement and growth which characterize them. The commentaries attempt to make sense out of particular elements of mystical experience by placing these in a comprehensive system of theological thought. They break into component parts the undifferentiated nature of that experience, so that these can be examined and related to the principles which undergird the analysis. What appears to be, at any moment within the system, a clearly-described phenomenon which is related to what has gone before and to what will follow is not experienced with such definition.

While a system is valuable in creating a logical and ordered sequence of analysis, it can appear to reduce what in life is experienced in complex and non-linear ways to cut-and-dried simplicities. It then becomes hard for the reader to identify with it, because questions like 'which point have I reached?' or 'have I completed the previous stage yet?' keep interfering with the reading. The system then becomes the meaning of the exercise, not a tool intended to clarify it. St John knew perfectly well that the inner life was not reducible to a bare system of universal application, certainly not one produced retrospectively, from the safety of the desired destination, union with God. He himself tells us on several occasions that God leads different souls by different paths, suggesting that there are likely to be as many different trajectories on the journey as there are souls who undertake it. It is therefore a misreading of St John to suppose that everyone must travel from A to B in a straight line, and the fact that between A and B he himself follows all kinds of twists and turns strongly suggests that he wanted to avoid creating such an impression and to demonstrate that the same journey could be looked at from many different points of view. That is why Teresa complements him so well, for her lack of formal theological training makes her especially aware of the dangers of too prescriptive an analysis.

The dynamism of the metaphor of the journey is important. Only one of his treatise titles show this: an ascent, obviously, is one kind of journey, because from the summit both the effort of the climb and the perspective of the route are transformed. But each of the others implies it. The 'Dark Night' poem recounts a night-time journey to union with the Beloved, and the night of the commentary is a dynamic and comprehensive symbol for the whole journey, from twilight through midnight towards dawn, as the opening of the *Ascent* already announces.[35] The 'Canticle' poem moves too, from a cry of pain caused by the

Beloved's absence through searching to union, while the commentary structures this movement according to the traditional threefold way of purgation, illumination and union. The flame of the *Living Flame* commentary is also dynamic, leaping upwards, an elemental and transforming force. St John does not describe a state but a process, a passing through and leaving behind of many states until the soul, in union with God, is free to realize at last her divine and human destiny through a reworking from within.

The analogy he most frequently uses to explain moments of crisis or transition in the journey is that of the child and parent, expressed in a number of different ways throughout the *Ascent* and *Dark Night*. It begins in the Prologue to the *Ascent* (3), where souls are hampered from making progress through inexperience or weakness, and stamp and cry like children who want to walk on their own feet before they have the strength, and resist their mothers' attempts to pick them up. The transition from meditation to contemplation is likened to weaning;[36] so too is his teaching on disregarding most kinds of physical visions, which he connects with Paul's contrast in 1 Cor. 13 between childish and adult experience.[37] The most extended use of the mother–child metaphor occurs at the beginning of the *Night*, and it acquires an increasing importance through the treatise:

> Once the soul has determined to be converted to the service of God, God ... nurtures it in spirit and cherishes it, like the loving mother with her tender babe, warming it by the warmth of her breasts, feeding it with nourishing milk and soft, sweet food, and carrying it in her arms and pampering it; but, as it grows, its mother starts removing her pampering, and, hiding her tender love, puts bitter aloes on her sweet breasts, and, lowering it from her arms, makes it walk on its own feet, so that as it loses the properties of a babe, it will be given to greater, more substantial things.[38]

This beautiful picture suggests that for maturity to be gained, a certain degree of independence is required, and that the process of gaining it sometimes leaves a bitter taste. It is that experience of pain to which the nights of the spirit correspond. Such is the work of 'the grace of God, our loving mother'. It certainly does

not support the notion of religion as a form of infantile dependence. The feminine imagery shows that a sixteenth-century
friar is perfectly capable of moving outside a patriarchal framework as far as the conception of God is concerned, and that such
language is firmly rooted in Christian tradition, and needs to be
recovered, not invented. The study of religious practices and of
the seven deadly sins is aimed at showing how childish religion
must be left behind, and is a hymn to inner humility, the one
essential virtue.

The terrors of the dark night are a necessary part of growth
towards union because they lead beginners from sensual kinds
of religion into the harsh way of the cross. This does not
happen without protest, just as babes complain when the
mother's breast is taken away;[39] but in this way, 'God, by
removing them from suckling at the breasts of these pleasures
and delights in pure interior dryness and darkness',[40] cures
them of their dependence and prepares them for the next
stage. The greatest of spiritual sufferings come in the passive
night of the spirit, but here supremely is the moment at which
those on the way begin to emerge at last from babyhood: 'God
senses that they are now beginning to grow up a little, and so
that they can grow stronger and come out of their baby
clothes, he puts them down from his arms and gets them used
to walking on their own feet, which feels very strange to them,
because everything has been reversed.'[41] When this image
returns[42] it stresses the distinction between drinking milk at
the breast and eating bread with the crust on, and links it with
the distinction between milk for babes and the solid food of
adults in Heb. 5.12–14. It is very clear that the passive night,
for all its language of negation, is a means to growth out of
infantile dependence on the toys and trinkets of spirituality,
towards a maturity which is capable of embracing the way of
the cross. St John uses other images to describe the journey
from the old and familiar to the new and strange, but, remembering perhaps his own mother's nurturing of abandoned
babies in Medina, finds in the processes of breast-feeding,
weaning and learning to walk unaided the loveliest picture of
all.

Reductionist analyses would claim that mystical experience,
especially when it expresses itself in erotic language, is a form of

sublimated sexuality. I doubt that either John's or Teresa's perceptiveness about the self can so readily be dismissed. It stems from too honest and painful an analysis of the self and the hidden forces which shape its behaviour. They teach detachment, not repression; that is, understanding why certain states and attitudes are obstacles to spiritual growth, rather than burying them in the unconscious; and their aim is the right kind of development towards wholeness and maturity in the soul, whose relationship with the exterior world of creatures is reordered in mutual freedom when she reaches union with God. It seems to me, as I reflect on these writers, that perhaps the true reason for their greatness as mystical theologians is that they hold together in creative tension the polar opposites of Christian doctrine and experience. They stand in awe before the transcendence of God, yet they affirm an intimacy of relationship with him. The humanity and the divinity of Christ are both essential; nor is there progress without struggle, resurrection without cross. They are individuals who are committed to community – one which seeks to incarnate the values of the gospel in a world which lives by different standards. John sets the journey of the individual soul within the whole Christian journey, by his use of Scripture, his stress on the way of the cross and his stern warnings against private revelations. But all their teaching must be read in the context of the Church's faith and its living out in the testing environment of small communities of believers, perhaps the most difficult environment of all in which to practise the love of neighbour. Nor is their writing individualistic: many times they touch on wider social questions, by exposing the vanity of the rich and the powerful, or simply by insisting on the primacy of love. The journey of any individual soul takes place within the redemptive work of the Trinity, while the whole of creation is the palace in which the Son will engage humanity to himself and take it as his Bride. If there is one thing missing, it is perhaps the note of fear, hell and damnation. It is present, but it is not appealed to, as so often in the period, to make humans love God. For as John himself wrote: where there is no love, put love, and you will receive love in return.

Notes

1. Rowan Williams, *Teresa of Avila* (London: Geoffrey Chapman, 1991), p. 43.
2. *From Ignatius Loyola to John of the Cross* (Variorum, 1995), VII, p. 287.
3. St Teresa, *Life*, 26.6.
4. Ibid., 4.6; 5.8; 12.2; 23.12.
5. Ibid., 14.7.
6. Ibid., 38.9.
7. Ibid., 9.7–8.
8. Alastair Hamilton, *Heresy and Mysticism in Sixteenth-Century Spain: The Alumbrados* (Cambridge: James Clarke, 1992), pp. 27–8.
9. Ibid., p. 29.
10. St Teresa, *Interior Castle*, 4.2.3.
11. Ibid., 4.2.7.
12. Ibid., 7.2.3.
13. Ibid., 7.4.6.
14. Ibid., 7.4.14.
15. Ibid., 7.4.10.
16. *San Juan de la Cruz: Obras completas*, ed. Eulogio Pacho (Burgos: Monte Carmelo, 1982), p. 129.
17. St John of the Cross, *Living Flame of Love*, 3.30–62. In this and the following paragraphs, works of St John of the Cross are referred to by initials commonly used in Spanish editions: C = *Spiritiual Canticle* (CA, first redaction; CB second redaction); L = *Living Flame of Love*; N = *Dark Night of the Soul*; S = *Ascent of Mount Carmel*.
18. St John of the Cross, *Ascent of Mount Carmel*, 1.2.
19. *San Juan de la Cruz: Obras completas*, ed. Lucinio Ruano de la Iglesia (11th edn, Madrid: Biblioteca de autores cristianos, 1982).
20. *Ascent*, 1.2.2.
21. Ibid., 1.2.3.
22. Ibid., 1.2.4.
23. Ibid., 1.2.5.
24. St John of the Cross, *Spiritual Canticle*, Prologue 3.
25. *Flame*, 3.30–62.
26. *Ascent*, 1.1–2.
27. Ibid., 1.3.3.
28. Ibid., 3.2.7.
29. *Ascent*, 1.13.1.
30. St John of the Cross, *The Dark Night of the Soul*, 2.5.3.
31. Ibid., 2.5.5.

32. Ibid., 2.5.6.
33. Ibid., 2.13.10.
34. Ibid., 2.9.1.
35. *Ascent*, 1.2.5.
36. Ibid., 2.14.3.
37. Ibid., 2.17.6.
38. *Night*, 1.2.
39. Ibid., 1.5.1.
40. Ibid., 1.7.5.
41. Ibid., 1.8.3.
42. Ibid., 1.12.1.

6

WILLIAM LAW AND THE WESLEYS

RON GLITHERO

I would like to consider William Law and the Wesley brothers very much as an interaction between two personalities, assuming for our immediate purpose that John and Charles Wesley did follow very similar patterns of spiritual development.

In 1777, by which time the Methodist Movement was well established, John Wesley issued *A Plain Account of Christian Perfection*, in which he looked back at the 1720s and the religious influences which were then strongest upon him.

> In the year 1725, being in the twenty-third year of my age, I met with Bishop Taylor's *Rule and Exercises of Holy Living and Dying*. In reading several parts of this book, I was exceedingly affected, that part in particular which relates to purity of intention. Instantly I resolved to dedicate all my life to God, all my thoughts, and words, and actions, being thoroughly convinced, there was no medium; but that every part of my life (not some only) must either be a sacrifice to God, or myself, that is, in effect, to the devil...
>
> In the year 1726, I met with Kempis's *Christian Pattern*. The nature and extent of inward religion, the religion of the heart, now appeared to me in a stronger light than ever it had done before. I saw that giving even all my life to God (supposing it possible to do this and go no farther) would profit me nothing, unless I gave my heart, yes all my heart to him. I saw that 'simplicity of intention, and purity of affection', one design in all we speak or do, and one desire ruling all our tempers, are indeed 'the wings of the soul', without which she can never ascend to the mount of God.
>
> A year or two after, Mr. Law's *Christian Perfection* and *Serious Call* were put into my hands. These convinced me more than ever of the absolute impossibility of being half a Christian. And I determined thro' his grace (the absolute

necessity of which I was deeply sensible of) to be all-devoted to God, to give him all my soul, my body, and my substance.[1]

Such was the influence which William Law's early writings had on Wesley during his formative years in Oxford. He wrote those words in 1777 after mature reflection. More immediately, in his Journal, in the preface to the entry for 24 May 1738, the day of his evangelical conversion, he wrote:

> But meeting now with Mr. Law's *Christian Perfection* and *Serious Call* they convinced me more than ever of the exceeding height and breadth and depth of the love of God. The light flowed in so mightily upon my soul that everything appeared in a new view. I cried to God for help and resolved not to prolong the time of obeying him, as I had never done before. And by my continued endeavor to keep his whole law, inward and outward, to the utmost of my power, I was persuaded that I should be accepted of him and that I was even then in a state of salvation.

In writing these words he recognized that he had moved beyond the limit, for him, of Law's spiritual guidance.

Let us now consider life at the Epworth Rectory where John and Charles Wesley were brought up, John being born there in 1703 and Charles in 1707. Their parents, Samuel and Susanna Wesley, were converts to Anglicanism from dissenting backgrounds. Samuel was a man of wide and serious reading, steeped in the sixteenth-century Puritan writers, the Caroline Divines of the seventeenth century, the Book of Common Prayer and the Authorized Version. John and Charles were reared in something of a spiritual hothouse, virtually isolated from the mainstream of contemporary life. Samuel Wesley remained Rector of Epworth because he was a thorn in the flesh of the Establishment; a High Churchman when High Churchmen were not in political or ecclesiastical favour; an 'exile' in the Isle of Axholme, where the fens were still in process of being drained. The Rectory was a home of serious study, devout feeling and rigid discipline.

In 1720 John went up to Christ Church, Oxford, as an intense, very serious young man. By 1725 he was preparing for ordination and began to feel that he should take his religious duties with greater seriousness. He was ready for his discovery of William Law.

William Law was born in 1686 in Kings Cliffe, Northamptonshire, where his father was a grocer. Very little is known about his early life save that by 1711 he was a Fellow of Emmanuel College, Cambridge. On the accession of George I in 1715 he refused to take the oath of allegiance to the Hanoverians. He was accordingly deprived of his Fellowship, and became associated with the Non-Jurors, and so increasingly isolated from the mainstream of Anglican life. In 1727 he became tutor to the Gibbon family in Putney, his particular charge being the father of Edward Gibbon, the author of *The Decline and Fall of the Roman Empire*. The Gibbons were a wealthy family, deeply involved in the radical religious thinking of the day and particularly impatient of any inherited orthodoxy. He was to stay with the family for a period of ten years, and this security of tenure would provide a stable background for the progress in his religious thinking.

He had already published *On Christian Perfection* in 1726 and *A Serious Call to a Devout and Holy Life* followed two years later. These two works had an immediate impact. They expressed a deep sense of spiritual commitment to the Christian faith. The beginning of the eighteenth century was a time of religious uncertainty, almost exhaustion, after the religious wars and conflicts of the previous century and Law's works were eagerly discussed in those local debating groups, philosophical societies and country rectories which were so much part of the English scene.

Edward Gibbon, the author of *The Decline and Fall*, came to be no friend of organized Christianity, but he could still comment: 'In our family, William Law left the reputation of a worthy and pious man who believed all that he professed, and practised all that he enjoined.'[2] And again:

Mr. Law's master-work, the *Serious Call* is still read as a popular and powerful book of devotion. His precepts are rigid, but they are founded on the Gospel: his satire is sharp; but it is drawn from the knowledge of human life; and many of his portraits are not unworthy of the pen of La Bruyere. If he finds a spark of piety in his reader's mind he will soon kindle it to a flame, and a Philosopher must allow, that he exposes with equal severity and truth, the strange contradiction between the faith and practise of the Christian World.[3]

Dr Samuel Johnson was also profoundly impressed:

I then became a sort of lax talker against religion, for I did not much think against it; and this lasted till I went to Oxford, when it would not be suffered. When at Oxford, I took up Law's Serious Call to a Holy Life, expecting to find it a dull book (as such books generally are), and perhaps to laugh at it. But I found Law quite an overmatch for me; and this was the first occasion of my thinking in earnest of religion, after I became capable of rational enquiry.[4]

Now we must see what it was about these two works which spoke so immediately to John Wesley at a critical period in his spiritual life. We will begin with a passage from *On Christian Perfection*.

Christianity is therefore a course of holy discipline, solely fitted to the cure and recovery of fallen spirits, and intends such a change in our nature, as may raise us to a nearer union with God, and qualify us for such high degrees of happiness ... That Christianity requires a change of nature, a new life perfectly devoted to God, is plain from the spirit and tenor of the gospel ... This new birth, this principle of a new life, is the very essence and soul of Christianity ... It is not therefore any number of moral virtues, no partial obedience, no modes of worship, no external acts of adoration, no articles of faith, but a new principle of life, an entire change of temper, that makes us true Christians.[5]

And again, when Law is speaking about nominal Christians:

But let such people remember, that they who thus measure themselves by themselves are not wise ... they are not members of Christ's mystical body, till they are united into him by a new spirit; that they have not entered into the kingdom of God, till they have entered with an infant simplicity of heart, till they are so born again as not to commit sin, so full of an heavenly spirit, as to have overcome the world.

Nothing less than this great change of heart and mind can give anyone any assurance, that he is truly turned to God.[6]

From *A Serious Call* Wesley found anticipation of the freedom of future Methodist patterns of discipline:

I take it for granted, that every Christian, that is in health, is up early in the morning; for it is much more reasonable to suppose a person is up early, because he is a Christian, than because he is a labourer, or a tradesman, or a servant, or has business that wants him ... how odious we must appear in the sight of heaven, if we are in bed, shut up in sleep and darkness, when we should be praising God ...

And if you are such a proficient in the spirit of devotion, that your heart is always ready to pray in its own language, in this case I press no necessity of borrowed forms ...

For though I think a form of prayer very necessary and expedient for public worship, yet if anyone can find a better way of raising his heart unto God in private, than by prepared forms of prayer, I have nothing to object against it ...

This seems to be the true liberty of private devotion; it should be under the direction of some form; but not so tied down to it, but that it may be free to take such new expressions, as its present fervours happen to furnish it with ...[7]

Law envisaged the possibility of perfect union with God through a life of disciplined and prayerful devotion. This was what Wesley wanted to hear. There followed several years of increasing spiritual intimacy. Then their ways were dramatically to diverge.

In 1729 Wesley was back in Oxford after two years as a curate in his father's parish. Then came the period of the Holy Club, founded by Charles, but soon organized by John. The Fellowship at Lincoln was resumed and in 1732 both brothers met with Law at the Gibbon household in Putney and a cordial sense of fellowship developed between them. In 1735 Samuel Wesley died, but John did not succeed to the Epworth living as he had hoped. The brothers joined Colonel Oglethorpe's expedition to found a settlement in Georgia. The

voyage was a stormy one and John was particularly impressed
with the courage and practical piety of a small group of Mora-
vians on board. The colonists in Georgia proved to be an undis-
ciplined lot. Not for them the Prayer Book discipline which
Wesley tried to impose. He enriched his services with readings
from Law which had so encaptured him, but to no avail. He
had wanted to preach to the Indians, but was kept well away
from them. By 1738 both brothers were back in England.

A brief visit to the Moravian settlement at Herrnhut was
quickly followed for John by the events of 24 May when, at a
Moravian meeting in Aldersgate Street, London, to which he
had gone very unwillingly, he felt his heart strangely warmed
and realized that Christ had taken away his sins, even his, and
had saved him from the law of sin and death. Charles had had a
similar experience a short time before, and had already written
a poem:

> Where shall my wondering soul begin?
> How shall I all to heaven aspire?
> A slave redeemed from death and sin,
> A brand plucked from eternal fire,
> How shall I equal triumphs raise,
> Or sing my great deliverer's praise?

There comes a powerfully evangelistic note:

> O how shall I the goodness tell,
> Father, which thou to me hast showed?

to be followed by:

> Outcasts of men, to you I call,
> Harlots, and publicans, and thieves!
> He spreads his arms to embrace you all;
> Sinners alone his grace receives.[8]

Here was the Evangelical Revival in verse. If we take these
words of Charles as echoing John's new spiritual experience,
then we see how the rigid approach to holiness of the previous
years has been suddenly shattered by this very profound
inward experience ... This is justification by faith vividly
expressed.

Meanwhile William Law was becoming fascinated by the

writings of Jacob Boehme (1575–1624) which had entered a period of popularity among the more exploratory religious circles of England and Scotland. Boehme was a Lutheran, deeply influenced by the mystics of his native Germany, with more than a trace of astrology and alchemy in his writings. In 1600 he had a religious experience on which he commented: 'What kind of spiritual triumph it was I can neither write nor speak: it can only be compared with that where life is born in the midst of death, and is like the resurrection of the dead.' For a period of fifteen minutes he believed that he

> Saw and knew the being of all beings, the ground and the unground; the birth of the holy Trinity; the source and origin of this world and all creatures in divine wisdom ... I saw three worlds in myself, 1. the divine, angelical, or paradisaical ... 2. the dark world ... 3. the external, visible world ... and I saw and knew the whole Being in evil and in good, how one originates in the other ... so that I not only greatly wondered but also rejoiced.[9]

He believed that he had been given this revelation for the benefit of the whole of mankind.

Law returned to Kings Cliffe in 1740 and remained there until his death in 1761. He set up a small community in the village, financially supported by two wealthy ladies, Hesther Gibbon, the sister of Edward Gibbon, and Mrs Hutchinson, 'put into Law's care' by her husband before his death. These two, together with Law, constituted a community with a rule and law of its own, but which never developed into anything bigger. They set up a school for girls in the village. They gave so generously to the poor that the Rector had to ask them to desist because layabouts from miles around were crowding into the village for what they could get. They gave money for a library and had engraved over its door the legend 'Books of Piety are here lent to any Persons of this or the neighbouring towns'.

Intellectually Law was still vigorous, and in the period 1749–54 his last two major works appeared, *The Spirit of Prayer* and *The Spirit of Love*. They showed a profound change in his thinking. Wesley could still find many 'great thoughts' there, but could not join Law in his journey into mysticism. The idea of absorption into the Godhead was too great a contrast to 'Bold, I approach the eternal Throne'.

The 1740s saw the extension of Methodist field-preaching, and the first local Methodist societies were set up. Preachers and local leaders had to be trained and supervised. Wesley was convinced of the need for practical rather than speculative theology, but his quest for holiness continued. He developed the Methodist teaching on Christian perfection: justification, leading to sanctification and on towards a perfection when one does love God with all one's heart, soul, mind, and strength, and one's neighbour as oneself.

What Methodism had to offer is emphasized in one of Charles Wesley's hymns not found in the current hymnbook and so lost to contemporary Methodism at congregational level:

> O come, ye sinners, to your Lord,
> In Christ to paradise restored;
> His proffered benefits embrace,
> The plenitude of Gospel grace:
>
> A pardon written with His blood,
> The favour and the peach of God,
> The seeing eye, the feeling sense,
> The mystic joys of penitence:
>
> The godly grief, the pleasing smart,
> The meltings of a broken heart,
> The tears that tell your sins forgiven,
> The sighs that waft your souls to heaven:
>
> The guiltless shame, the sweet distress,
> The unutterable tenderness,
> The genuine, meek humility
> The wonder – Why such love to me?
>
> The o'erwhelming power of saving grace
> The sight that veils the seraph's face;
> The speechless awe that dares not move,
> And all the silent heaven of love.[10]

Rather more widely known is the final verse of 'Love divine, all loves excelling':

Finish then thy new creation,
    Pure and spotless let us be;
Let us see thy great salvation
    Perfectly restored in thee;
Changed from glory into glory,
    Till in heaven we take our place,
Till we cast our crowns before thee
    Lost in wonder, love, and praise![11]

In 1756 John Wesley wrote an open letter to William Law, showing that he had parted company from his former mentor, describing him elsewhere as a mystic, who denies justification by faith. The letter was unexpected: its immediate context unknown. Soon afterwards Law wrote to 'a person of quality', almost certainly Selina, Countess of Huntingdon, a leading evangelical of the time:

I once was a kind of oracle with Mr. Wesley. I never suspected anything bad of him, or even discovered any kind, or degree of falseness, or hypocrisy in him. But during all the time of his intimacy with me, I judged him to be much under the power of his own spirit, which seemed to have the predominancy in every good thing, or way, that his zeal carried him to.[12]

'Wesley under the power of his own spirit.' Perhaps there was something of that in the way in which his own followers could refer to him, in his later years, as 'Pope John'.

Notes

1. John Wesley, *A Plain Account of Christian Perfection* 1777, from Wesley's *Works*, Vol. XI, pp. 366–7, quoted in J. Brazier Green, *John Wesley and William Law* (London: Epworth Press, 1956), p. 29.
2. Edward Gibbon, *Miscellaneous Works*, vol. 1, p. 14, quoted in Brazier Green, *Wesley and Law*, p. 43.
3. Edward Gibbon, *Memoirs of My Life*, ed. Georges A. Bonnard (London: Nelson, 1966), pp. 22–3.
4. James Boswell, *Life of Johnson* (Everyman edn; Dent, 1922), vol. 1, pp. 32–3, quoted in Brazier Green, *Wesley and Law*, p. 43.
5. *The Works of Rev William Law*. Vol. III, *A Practical Treatise upon*

Christian Perfection, 1726, privately printed for G. Moreton, Brockenhurst, 1893, p. 25.

6. Ibid., p. 35.
7. *Works*, Vol. IV, *A Serious Call to a Devout and Holy Life, adapted to the State and Condition of all Orders of Christians*, ch. 14, Moreton, pp. 128, 135.
8. Charles Wesley, *Hymns and Psalms* (London: Methodist Publishing House, 1983), no. 706.
9. Quoted in Brazier Green, *Wesley and Law*, p. 100.
10. *Methodist Hymn Book* (London: Methodist Conference Office, 1933), no. 325.
11. Charles Wesley, *Hymns and Psalms*, no. 267.
12. *Works*, Vol. IX, *A Collection of Letters* 1760, Moreton, Letter VIII, pp. 168–9.

7

SPIRITUALITY AND UNITY

RALPH WALLER

In this chapter I want to trace the impact of the catholic spirituality of Richard Baxter on the Methodists of the eighteenth century and the Unitarians of the nineteenth century.

John Wesley was influenced by the spirituality and catholicity of Richard Baxter, largely though the impact of his mother, Susanna Wesley. Susanna's father, Dr Samuel Annesley, was a Dissenter. He deserves a place in the record of English history, if for no other reason, by virtue of the fact that he was the father of 25 children (by two marriages), the youngest of whom was Susanna Wesley. It is interesting to speculate that if Susanna had only had 17 children then there would have been no Charles Wesley and Methodism and indeed the wider Church would have been deprived of many of its greatest hymns. However, if Dr Annesley had been the father of only 24 children then there would have been no Methodism at all.

Dr Samuel Annesley was a leading dissenting minister and a close friend of Richard Baxter. Wesley's sermon on 'The Catholic Spirit', first preached in Newcastle in 1749, shows clearly the influence of Richard Baxter. Having said that he does not wish to enter into doctrinal disputes on minor matters, Wesley goes on to say, 'If you love God and your fellow man, give me your hand'.

Like other dissenting ministers, Dr Annesley had been ejected from office in 1662, but unlike many other Dissenters the wealth he had inherited had enabled him to live without a stipend and therefore gave him a great deal of freedom. His grandfather had been a peer of the realm and his uncle, the Earl of Anglesey, was a Privy Councillor.

Samuel Annesley entered Queen's College, Oxford at the age of 15. He was ordained in 1644 and served as a minister of the Church of England at Gravesend, from where he moved into the City of London to be the Rector of St John's Church in Friday Street and then of St Giles in Cripplegate. It was from there that he published a volume of sermons he had preached, entitled *The Morning Exercises of Cripplegate*, whose main theme was that of a life guided by the conscience; this work came to hold an important place in Puritan literature. After he was ejected from his living he continued to preach in London and also used part of the fortune that he had inherited from his father's estate to support dissenting ministers who were in difficulties. For 30 years, until his death in 1696, his home was a central meeting place for London dissent. It is my contention that through him, Baxter's spirituality and catholicity were communicated via Susanna to John and Charles Wesley.

John Wesley's sermon on 'The Catholic Spirit' shows that Wesley, following the nonconformity of his mother and of the seventeenth-century divine, Richard Baxter, came to believe that the Christian faith could never be fully encapsulated in any form of words. He recognized that people's apprehensions, experiences and temperaments differed from person to person, and that these differences produced varied dogmatic conceptions of the faith; moreover Wesley held that, while it was important for everyone to follow his or her own inclinations in regard to the truth, these should not be the cause of hostility against those holding different views.

> Every wise man will allow others the same liberty of thinking which he desires they should allow him; and will not more insist on their embracing his opinions, than he would have them to insist on his embracing theirs. He bears with those who differ from him, and only asks him with whom he desires to unite in love that single question, 'Is thy heart right, as my heart is with thy heart?' ... I do not mean embrace my modes of worship, or I will embrace yours. This also is a thing which does not depend either on your choice or mine. We must both act as each is persuaded in his own mind. Hold fast to that which you believe is most acceptable to God, and I will do the same. I believe the Episcopal form of Church Government to be scriptural and apostolical. If you think the Presbyterian or Independent is better, think so still, and act accordingly. I believe infants ought to be baptised; and that this may be done either by dipping or

sprinkling. If you are otherwise persuaded, be still so, and follow your own persuasion. It appears to me that forms of prayer are of excellent use, particularly in the great congregations. If you judge extemporary prayer to be of more use, act suitably to your own judgement. My sentiment is, that I ought not to forbid water, wherein persons may be baptised; and that I ought to eat bread and drink wine as a memorial of my dying Master; however, if you are not convinced of this, act according to the light you have. I have no desire to dispute with you one moment upon any of the preceding heads. Let all these smaller points stand aside. Let them never come into sight. 'If thine heart is as my heart,' if thou lovest God and all mankind, I ask no more: 'Give me thine hand.'[1]

This sermon shows a remarkable breadth of sympathy on Wesley's part towards those who advocated a very different churchmanship from his own; it also has important implications for spirituality and unity.

Wesley gives a glimpse of three insights which together make a major contribution to the spirituality of the Christian Church. These insights are: 1. the Church centred on Christ; 2. the Church as a community; and 3. the diversity of the catholic Church. The first idea, of the Church centred on Christ, shows that for Wesley the basis of Christian fellowship was not agreement on doctrine, but an allegiance to the person of Christ. The second and third concepts, of the Christian community and its diversity, are indications of Wesley's belief that the Church was not simply made up of individuals but in its essence has a communal nature which is enhanced and enriched by diversity and variety.

JESUS CHRIST IS CENTRAL TO THE CHURCH

In his sermon on 'The Catholic Spirit' Wesley asks a central question, 'Dost thou believe in the Lord Jesus Christ?' For Wesley the centre of the Church is Jesus Christ and the discussion of the Church starts from this point. The Church is defined by its centre, Christ. The very word 'Church' invariably assumes discipleship to Christ. It is not the story of Jesus, nor his picture, nor his doctrine that is central to the Church, but the person of Christ himself. Where the person is supposed to be unreal the faith itself cannot be real. To the relationship between master and disciple both parties are indispensable; and if the master vanishes into a figment of the imagination, then the disciple slides into pretence. But it is Christ whose personality can be seen in what Karl Barth called 'the mirror of the narrative' who is the inspiration of the Church. Moreover Christ is the external standard of all that is sacred and holy against which individual beliefs, experiences and interpretations can be tested. He is the one who prevents religion from being merely a private and subjective belief; he brings harmony into it and reaffirms the true inner revelations of God. For Wesley the Church was a gathering of the Lord's disciples. Without Christ the community would cease to be a Church. St Ignatius put this theme in words of great significance: 'Where Christ is there is his Church.' The Church can be defined as a circle with the centre, Jesus Christ, but it is also a circle without a clearly defined circumference which would make it exclusive, or indeed without any segments that would separate the denominations. All the reference points are taken from the centre, Jesus Christ. This open nature of the Church arises from the fact that Christ is the head; he unites his disciples and awakens them to the presence of the family of God.

Christian communities are not essentially made by agreement on rules and regulations, but by shared memories and thoughts, desires, sympathies and love. At the heart of Christian spirituality is common worship, prayer and singing of hymns, and above all, sharing the sacrament of Holy Communion. At the heart of catholicity lies no dogmatic system, but spiritual affections towards God and towards humanity. This is the key principle for a truly catholic Church; a union of holiness and love, founded on and inspired by Jesus Christ.

THE CHURCH AS THE CHRISTIAN COMMUNITY

This approach to Christian doctrine may leave the impression of being concerned simply with the individual and his relationship to God, facilitated through Jesus Christ. This is not the case. The Church also has to be considered as a corporate body, with a strong sense of the Christian community.

Wesley's phrase, 'If thou lovest God and all mankind, I ask no more: Give me thine hand,' is symbolic of this fellowship. Wesley could argue from a theological basis, and from a practical point of view, against an individualism which undermines the corporate nature of the Church. On theological grounds Wesley argues that a Christian's life is not his or her own to do with as he or she wills, but that we belong to a holy society, and have a responsibility towards other members of the community. It must also be recognized that the individual's conscience and inner feelings are not the only factors that determine Christian behaviour; respect is also needed for the consciences of others.

From a practical point of view, it could be maintained that very few people thoroughly believe or disbelieve alone by themselves, but that they usually need the sympathy of others to confirm their own inner feelings. If our beliefs and feelings are not confirmed by others then we might well begin to suspect that we are deluded. In this way faith is not simply an individual property, but is much more a process of catholic consent. Religion can never be a purely individual experience between the worshipper and God; it is much more a relationship connecting individuals with each other and with God.

The Christian Church is not limited simply to an earthly fellowship, but contains an historical community of former generations linked to those living in the present, and a community in heaven which is joined to Christians on earth. This total church community is made possible by Christ and held together by him. St Paul's thought of one family distributed between heaven and earth (Eph. 3.14–15) is a key theme for the doctrine of the Church. It is Christ who united those in heaven and on earth in one family, and it is his spirit which draws people together in the community of the Church. Any serious study of the Church produces an awareness that much has been inherited from the past and that we owe a debt to great Christians of former ages. This continuity is found especially through the singing of hymns and psalms that have been left by former generations as a record of their communion with God. Through them we can identify with the confessions and struggles and desires of those who lived in a previous age, and gain inspiration from the past.

THE CATHOLIC CHURCH AND ITS DIVERSITY

The idea of catholicity within the Church ought to begin with the observation that there are real differences in people's perceptions of the Christian faith, and that these differences actually enrich the faith. Wesley encouraged his hearers not to give up beliefs which apparently tended to divide the Christian Church, but he instructed them to 'hold you fast to that which you believe is most acceptable to God'. These are not superficial differences, or the results of unfortunate accidents, but they lie in the very nature of humanity and are intrinsic to the life of the Church, which would be immeasurably impoverished without them.

This true union among Christian people does not depend upon similarity of thought but will often include a wide variety of opinion. In the same way as in magnetism unlike poles attract each other, so too in this union, those who hold diverse views can live in harmony and sympathy with one another. Many of us could illustrate this fact from our own lives, being conscious that our greatest spiritual inspiration is often come from writers not of our own denomination. This practice of drawing from a wide catholic background is also influential in worship. Although Wesley did not agree with Toplady's theology he still included his hymn 'Rock of Ages cleft for me' in his hymn books.

The issues we have discussed – the Church centred on Christ, the communal aspect of the Church, and its diversity – arise out of Wesley's view of the catholic spirit; but it is also one of the strong points of his theology that he recognized that a true catholic spirit cannot be retained in the narrow confines of the Church but must reach out into the wider community. Towards the end of his sermon he wrote of the Christian:

> But while he is steadfastly fixed in his religious principles, in what he believes to be the truth as it is in Jesus; while he firmly adheres to that worship of God which he judges to be most acceptable in His sight; and while he is united by the tenderest and closest ties to one particular congregation – his heart is enlarged towards all mankind, those he knows and those he does not; he embraces with strong and cordial affection neighbours and strangers, friends and enemies.

This is catholic or universal love. And he that has this is of the catholic spirit.[2]

The English Presbyterians of the nineteenth century

Nineteenth-century English theology and church life was dominated by the Anglicans. Successive waves of influence from the Anglican Evangelicals, the Broad Church and the High Church movements swept across the religious life of the nation. The dominant figures of the age were also Anglicans: Coleridge, F. D. Maurice, Newman and Pusey, and Keble, Temple, and Illingworth and Gore.

The century is also noted for the re-emergence of Roman Catholicism in England, and of course for the growth of some of the major Nonconformist denominations, led by Methodism, but closely followed by the Congregationalists and the Baptists, with Spurgeon preaching his way out of the back streets and speaking to the nation. And towards the end of the century we see Scottish Presbyterianism following on the heels of Scotsmen moving south into England in search of work. However, one denomination whose history is often overlooked is that of the English Presbyterians, who towards the end of the eighteenth century and the beginning of the nineteenth century were moving away from orthodoxy towards Arianism and on to Unitarianism. This small group of congregations, largely made up of the English Presbyterians, but added to by defectors from Congregationalism, such as Priestley, and deserters from the Anglican Church, such as Lindsey and Price, deserves to be more closely studied, for it exerted a more powerful influence on the religious life of the nation than is sometimes realized. These congregations did much to promote biblical research and critical investigation, and they were instrumental in the founding of many of the new universities of the nineteenth century: University College, London, Liverpool and Manchester Universities, Nottingham and Leicester University Colleges, and of course, Manchester College, Oxford. In addition to these educational achievements they kept in close contact with the intellectual life of Germany and Scotland at a time when the ancient universities of Oxford and Cambridge were somewhat inward looking. Nineteenth-century English

Unitarians promoted modern christological studies, ethics, hymnology and liturgy, and they exerted a profound influence upon many of the leading thinkers of the day. In the Unitarian Chapel at Shrewsbury there is a plaque in the pulpit commemorating the fact that Coleridge preached there on three successive winter Sundays while candidating for the post of Junior Minister. There is another plaque on the wall of the same chapel reminding us that Darwin was a boy in the Sunday School. Fredrick Denison Maurice grew up in a Unitarian home, and throughout his life held a profound respect for his father who was a Unitarian minister. Francis Newman, the brilliant brother of John Henry Newman, became a Unitarian, and Jabez Bunting, the architect of the modern Methodist Church, grew up in the home of a kindly Unitarian doctor. At one time all the city councillors of Nottingham were Unitarian. English Presbyterians such as Thomas Percival and Southwood Smith pioneered medical ethics and community medicine. The brilliant Unitarian, James Martineau, exercised a powerful influence on a whole generation of Anglicans through his classes and published sermons and addresses; these included Bishop Colenso, F. W. Robertson (the greatest of nineteenth-century preachers), Stopford Brook (the writer and preacher), Catherine Winkworth (the translator of Luther's hymns), and Anna Swanwick (who helped in the founding of Bedford College, London; Girton College, Cambridge and Somerville College, Oxford). And when the religion and science debate was at its height, James Martineau was seen, even by orthodox Anglicans, as a champion of faith. And yet this tradition, with its liberal influences, is hardly known and little acknowledged.

They also made an important contribution to spirituality.

John James Tayler

John James Tayler (1797–1869), Unitarian minister and Principal of Manchester College, was born on 15 August 1797 at Church Row, Newington Butts in Surrey. He was the elder son of James Tayler (1765–1831), a Nonconformist minister. In 1814 John James Tayler was sent to train for the Unitarian ministry at Manchester College, York, under the Principalship of Charles Wellbeloved. A letter written by Tayler at this time records that he was learning Greek, Hebrew, Arabic and Mathematics, all in the same week. His days at Manchester College were happy ones, but at the close of his second year he left York and spent the following two years at the University of Glasgow reading for a BA degree. He was awarded the degree in 1819 and straightaway returned to Manchester College as a temporary assistant tutor in classics, while his old tutor John Kenrick was in Germany studying with Schleiermacher.

The year spent as a tutor changed the course of his life. He had previously hoped to study medicine and combine the duties of a minister with those of a doctor. However, the financial difficulties of a long medical training, combined with his increasing interest in theology, caused him to abandon the idea. Thus in 1820 at the age of 23 he accepted an invitation to become the minister of Mosley Street Chapel, Manchester; and on 16 January 1825 married Hannah, the daughter of Timothy Smith of Icknield.

Like his contemporaries, the members of the Oxford Movement, Tayler was also influenced by Romanticism. From his published correspondence, which is a little cameo of Victorian intellectual life, it can be seen that as a student of Glasgow he was avidly reading Scott, and on one of his early visits to the Lake District he joined Wordsworth for tea and the two men went for a long walk together later in the week. Further influence of the Romantic Movement on Tayler can be seen by the fact that in 1839 Sir Charles Barry, the architect of the new Houses of Parliament, was commissioned, amid controversy, but with Tayler's approval, to build the new Upper Brook Street Chapel in a splendid Gothic style. This move away from the rectangular and octagonal chapels which were light, airy and conducive to rationalism, towards Gothic-style churches with stained-glass windows, choir pews and high altars which were never used, was a reflection of the moving of Unitarian thought from an excessive reliance upon rationalism, as propounded by Joseph Priestley, towards a more spiritual and romantic religion in which devotion to Christ was central. Tayler achieved this revolution within Unitarianism, partly through his joint editorship of the influential *Prospective Review* and partly through his control of Manchester College, which was the sole institution for the training of Unitarian ministers.

In 1840 Manchester College moved back to Manchester from York, with an enlarged staff and with a determination to become a small university. Tayler was appointed Professor of Ecclesiastical History, with James Martineau as Professor of Philosophy and Francis Newman as Professor of Classics. Tayler continued his ministry at Upper Brook Street, holding the two posts in tandem until 1853 when the College moved to London and he was appointed Principal of the new institution, a post he held until his death in 1869. Tayler fought vigorously for Church unity within a wider state church, on the grounds that such a unity would not duplicate resources but would encourage a highly trained ministry, strengthen the parochial system and enable Christians to unite in social action. He strongly advocated this position in his publication *A Catholic Christian Church, the Want of our Time* (1867).

THE GRAND SCHEME OF UNION

On Friday afternoon on 14 June 1867 John James Tayler, with a group of approximately seventy people, met in the Library of Manchester New College, in Gordon Square, London. Tayler was one of the leaders for a grand scheme of Christian union. The circular which advertised the meeting gave the following purpose of the assembly: 'To consider the means of forming a closer union among Liberal Christian Churches and persons, for the promotion and application of religion in life, apart from doctrinal limitations in thought.' The name Free Christian Union was chosen, but only after much discussion as to whether the word 'Christian' should be included or not. J. J. Tayler intimated that he would probably not have joined the Union if the word Christian had been omitted from the title for such a society would be so aimless and so incapable of any practical religious issue.[3] Martineau along with Tayler also strongly defended the inclusion of the word 'Christian'.[4]

The union was not to be formed by assent to a minimum doctrinal standard, but was to rest upon a much more pragmatic basis, in refusing to insist on anything other than that which was necessary to fulfil the simple conditions of common worship and work. In Tayler's own words it sought 'religious sympathies rather than theological agreement'.[5]

Both Tayler and Martineau worked hard to promote the new body. Martineau wrote an impressive work entitled, *New Affinities of Faith: A Plan for a Free Christian Union* (1869) in which he carefully set out the aims of the Union and met point by point some of the criticisms with which it had been assailed.[6] 'A fine paper for the Free Christian Union' was Henry Sidgwick's comment on Martineau's work, in a letter written to his mother on 8 February 1869.[7] Tayler did his best to promote the enterprise in his booklet entitled, *A Catholic Christian Church, the Want of Our Time* (1867).

Tayler, Martineau and Sidgwick, the Cambridge philosopher, were the key people behind the Union. The Revd Kegan Paul, the Vicar of Sturminster Marshall, Dorset, also became a prominent member, and Tayler persuaded M. Athanase Coqueel of the French Protestant Church to be actively involved.[8] At the end of the first year the movement appeared to be gaining momentum, and the room taken for the anniversary service was far too small for the large gathering, so the meeting had to be adjourned while large premises were found.

The Inquirer, which covered the opening meeting of the Union in 1867 in an article of some five thousand words, was not permitted to report the anniversary meeting of 1868. The editor of *The Inquirer* was annoyed by the chairman's statement at the commencement of the proceedings that the meeting was strictly private. The editor had learned that the reason for this privacy was due to the presence of some Broad Churchmen who were willing to address the gathering but did not wish their remarks to be reported; an attitude which he thoroughly condemned.[9]

Nevertheless, after being in existence for a year the movement was growing and gathering support. In November of 1868 Tayler wrote to his friend, John Hamilton Thom, to seek his advice as the question of whether or not to drop Christian from the title of the Union had arisen again with the publication of Francis Newman's pamphlet, *Against Hero Making in Religion* (1868). Tayler's own view, expressed in this letter, remained unchanged:

If we throw off the Christian name, we shall lose the sympathy of myriads of devout and spiritual minded men,

111

who will be thrown back by an instinctive conservation on narrow dogmatic views as the only salvation, as they think, of a vital faith. After all, what *practical* object do we gain, by widening our limits to take in Jews, Mahomedans, Parsees, Brahmins, Confucians etc? ... There are excellent men in all these religions, whose acceptance with God I have no more doubt of, than I have of good Christians. But why not leave them to work out the function assigned them by Providence in their own sphere – encouraging and rejoicing in their social progress, but not annoying and interrupting them by a fussy and narrow proselytism – we ourselves limiting our immediate endeavours to the development of a higher spiritual life in Christian Europe?[10]

While in writing to J. H. Thom, Tayler is defending the need for the Free Christian Union to limit its activities and sphere of influence to Christianity; in a subsequent letter he goes on to argue for the Union to compass a truly broad and catholic (meaning comprehensive) spectrum of the Church. In his letter to the Revd Athanase Coqueel of Paris he maintained that

The Union must recognise the freedom of each individual to hold his own opinions on doctrinal and speculative subjects. However, on matters, such as, common worship, Christian labour, and mutual recognition of Christian brethren a more inclusive nature should be sought, based upon religious sympathy rather than in theological agreement.[11]

M. Coqueel did accept Tayler's invitation to preach at a service of the Free Christian Union on 1 June 1869, but unfortunately Tayler died three days before the event. Within a year of Tayler's death the movement was disbanded.

There were several reasons for failure. In the first place the Union had failed to capture the hearts and minds of the clergy of the Church of England and of University tutors. A letter from Sidgwick following his conversations at Oxford highlights this problem:

I talked to Jowett. He is by no means unsympathetic and was anxious not to discourage the undertaking. But he seems to think 1) that Anglican clergymen ought to take the Church of England for their sphere of liberalising work: 2) that the union between enlightened Christians of all denominations though very real, was too ethereal to be expressed in the concrete form of an association.[12]

There were other factors which caused the failure of the Union. One of the major aims of the Union was that of 'common action' but worthwhile projects for common action did not readily suggest themselves. However, the main factor for the failure of the Union was Tayler's death soon after his return from Transylvania in 1869. With Tayler's death was removed the one person who had the ability to hold the enterprise together and bring it out of obscurity into the public view. Martineau, although an able man, did not have the practical and political skills to promote the movement.

Tayler's theological contribution to the movement, *The Catholic Church: The Want of Our Time*, is important in that it reveals some of the essential pictures of his spirituality, his ecclesiology and his ideas on ecumenism. Tayler commences the work by stating that he held the essence of Christianity is to be found in the spiritual principles of 'love, trust and immortal hope'. He further believed that a true catholic Church would be based on these principles and could only be formed by a union of holiness and love. He expressed sadness that the Reformers selected as a true test of Christianity the very things on which people differ, theological opinions which were often transitory modes of religious thought, rather than on common sympathies of love, reverence, holiness and trust.[13]

Tayler did not belittle theology; indeed he felt that every individual had to have a theology, but he recognized theology as an attempt to put into human formulas the conclusions of speculative thought. As such he saw theology as something with which individuals were concerned; that it was transitory and changing, while in contrast to the individual the Church was concerned with what was universal and eternal. He was trying to establish the essence of Christianity but not in the sense of a minimal belief held in common by the many. Tayler's essence of Christianity is located in devotion to Christ and in the common practical religion of the Christian life.

Tayler was unusual among Nonconformists in that he was

clearly in favour of a national church. Most Nonconformists at this time were fighting for disestablishment and for their own denominational interests. Tayler gave four reasons for supporting a united national church. In the first place, he recognized that a national church would be able to use resources widely and not duplicate them. Secondly, he believed that a national church would be able to provide excellent ministerial training. Ministers from different traditions would be educated together as in Holland and Germany. It was also his experience that it was possible to find a deep spiritual sympathy with someone from a different church background. Thirdly, he felt that there were many benefits of the parochial system. Fourthly, he felt that if Churches were united there would be a stronger base for united social action.[14]

James Martineau

James Martineau (1805–1900) was born on 21 April 1805, the seventh child of a middle-class merchant family of Norwich. The home had its own invigorating atmosphere. There were eight children, and the older children played their part in the formal education of the younger: Thomas, the eldest, taught Latin; Elizabeth taught French, and Henry, writing and arithmetic. All this activity took place with the enthusiastic support of their parents, who knew the importance of discerning encouragement in education. James later said of his father that he was always ready to strain every nerve to advance the education of his children.

From 1815 to 1819 Martineau was a day pupil at the public grammar school in the cathedral close. The headmaster of the time was Edward Valpy. There were some 230 pupils in the school, several of whom rose in later life to prominence in civil and military life: they included James Brooke the Rajah of Sarawak, George Borrow the writer, and Edward Rigby and John Dalrymple who became eminent in the field of medicine. However his school days were not happy as he suffered bullying and moreover felt frustrated, the ethos of the school being centred on classics and grammar, whereas his interest lay in the direction of mathematics and science. His unhappiness came to an end through the intervention of his sister, Harriet, who returned to Norwich full of enthusiasm for the classes of Dr Lant Carpenter that she had attended in Bristol. Thomas Martineau provided the 100 guineas a year to meet the fees and enrolled James in Dr Lant Carpenter's School.

Lant Carpenter carried his wide range of interests with him into the classroom; he was a man of the world who read the daily papers to the pupils around the dinner table and kept them in touch with the Parliamentary debates. He encouraged his pupils to start their own debating society and to care for the poor from their own funds. He laid great stress on moral and religious education, and introduced his pupils to contemporary biblical criticism. The school curriculum at Bristol included lessons in science, history, geography and in the Greek Testament, as well as in classics and mathematics. This curriculum widened Martineau's horizons and gave him a foundation which enabled him to cope with the scientific revolution of the nineteenth century. Even more important than the subject matter and the patterns of thought developed at Bristol, was the immediate influence of the man. Lant Carpenter was both a deeply religious man and a profound thinker, and his spirit stayed with Martineau for the rest of his life.

On the completion of his schooling in the autumn of 1821, the family set out for a holiday in the Lake District. They stayed with friends near Cockermouth. The view of the distant mountains with their sunny knolls and dark hollows filled James with wonder. It awakened within him a love of mountaineering and like many other of his time he found a new world in the world of beauty and nature.

In 1822, against his father's advice, who had warned him he was courting poverty, but who nevertheless found the money to support him, he entered Manchester College, York to train for the ministry. The members of the Manchester College staff, Charles Wellbeloved, John Kenrick and William Turner were all competent men. It was the admirable teaching of Turner which gave fresh impetus to Martineau's mathematical studies and enabled him to attain an ambition of reading Newton's *Principia*. He greatly admired the Principal, Charles Wellbeloved, and from him received not only the principles of sound biblical criticism, but also an overriding view of the catholicity of the Church. John Kenrick had just returned from studying

115

with Schleiermacher in Berlin, and shared with his pupils the results of his recently gained knowledge. He and Martineau became life-long friends.

In the summer of 1828, after one year in Bristol, Martineau accepted the post of Junior Minister of Eustace Street Presbyterian Meeting House, Dublin, with the Revd Joseph Hutton, grandfather of Richard Holt Hutton, as his colleague. At the end of the year he married Helen Higginson of Derby, and settled down to his teaching and ministerial work with the hope of a long and fruitful stay in Dublin. In the event his ministry lasted under four years owing to his refusal to accept any part of the Regium Donum, the annual grant bestowed by Parliament on Presbyterian Ministers. During his Dublin years he published *A Collection of Hymns for Christian Worship* (1831). The book contained 273 hymns, five of which were by his sister Harriet. Martineau drew his hymns from a wider spiritual tradition than had many previous compilers of Unitarian and Non-Subscribing Presbyterian hymn books, with the hymns of Isaac Watts and Bishop Hever well represented.

In the summer of 1832 the Martineaus left their first home, said farewell to their friends, stood in silence together in the French churchyard by the little grave of their firstborn, and then crossed the sea with a son and a daughter to Liverpool to enter upon the most formative and productive period of James's life.

Martineau took up the position of minister of Paradise Street Chapel. It was here that he formed a close association with J. H. Thom and Charles Wicksteed of Liverpool and J. J. Tayler of Manchester. They were aided by Joseph Blanco White, the turbulent Spanish Roman Catholic priest, who became an Anglican and member of the Oriel College Senior Common Room before being introduced by Thom into Liverpool Unitarian circles. For several years, while editing the *Prospective Review* the four friends met once a month at Tayler's home. They dined, spent their evening together, and often stayed overnight. These were memorable occasions for all of them, and they interacted in a special way to stimulate and promote one another's thoughts.

In 1836 Martineau published a remarkable little book under the title *The Rationale of Religious Inquiry* which went into four editions and indeed was republished after his death under the title *What is Christianity?* The impact of this book was extensive, especially in America where according to the Harvard Tutor, Joseph Henry Allen, it was responsible for starting the Transcendental Movement in the American Free Churches. As far as English theology was concerned it was an important attempt to examine Christianity philosophically. In the Preface Martineau maintained that religion and philosophy had traditionally occupied different spheres with little or no contact between them, except in the field of natural religion. Martineau published this volume in the hope of providing an improved philosophical method for investigating Christianity, namely that religious truth must not be contrary to reason. Martineau was not advocating that the Christian faith must lie within the limits of reason, but rather that, although it goes beyond what reason can prove, it does not go against reason. He expressed this in the phrase, 'A divine right, therefore, to dictate a perfectly unreasonable faith cannot exist'. In the development of Martineau's religious thought there were two movements taking place at this time: one was towards a more critical approach to the Scriptures and religious tradition, while the other was towards a religion based on feeling which emphasized worship and devotion to Christ. Both these elements can be found within *The Rationale*, although the critical element dominates. The Wesleyan Conference, meeting the following year, was urged to make special appointments to Liverpool to refute the brilliant Martineau.

During his remaining seventeen years in Liverpool, Martineau wrote some 45 major articles and contributed to several nineteenth-century journals as well as producing his outstanding hymn book *Hymns for the Christian Church and Home* (1840) and his fine collection of sermons, *Endeavours after the Christian Life* (1843). The former, which drew from a wide variety of Christian spirituality, exerted a powerful influence on English Unitarianism becoming the most widely used hymn book in the movement. The latter had a powerful influence outside English Unitarianism. It was avidly read by Anglicans such as John Colenso and F. W. Robertson and its ideas and images were often reproduced in their sermons.

It was during his ministry at Liverpool that Martineau

started his classes for young ladies. Among those to benefit from his teaching were Catherine and Suzanna Winkworth, and Anna Swanwick, who felt grateful for the rest of her life to Martineau for his assistance and guidance in her youth; their friendship continued over the following 65 years.

During the 1840s Martineau began to feel that the Paradise Street Church building, conducive to eighteenth-century rationalism, was inappropriate for his new theological emphasis. Like the members of the Oxford Movement he too had been affected by Romanticism. Hope Street Church was accordingly built in 1848 to rehouse the congregation. It was a beautiful Victorian-Gothic building, with statues, stained glass windows, choir pews and a high altar that was never used but which helped to create an atmosphere of medieval gloom, conducive to Martineau's ethereal voice and aesthetic sermons.

Martineau succeeded Tayler as Principal of Manchester College and held the post until his eightieth birthday in 1885. In the year following the formation of the Free Christian Union Martineau was involved in the foundation of the Metaphysical Society. The original plan drawn up by Dean Stanley, Archbishop Manning and Mr Knowles was to form a society of believers to discuss questions of theology and to refute agnostics. When Martineau was approached to join, he said that he had no wish to belong to a society of 'gnostics to put down agnostics'. At his insistence the plan was enlarged to form a society comprehending all schools of thought, theological and scientific. Its membership included John Tyndall, Thomas Huxley and Alfred Tennyson. In this influential society he formed many friendships.

The nineteenth-century debate on science and religion is often portrayed by the famous confrontation between Huxley and Wilberforce which took place in the University Museum in Oxford. Although this encounter captured the public imagination, it can be argued that the major battle of the conflict between science and religion was not centred on Huxley and Wilberforce but on the debate of 1872 between James Martineau and Professor John Tyndall. Martineau's campaign was largely defensive and concentrated on two fundamental issues. He argued against matter being self-sufficient, able to create and construct out of its own necessity, and thus removing the need for God; and he vigorously opposed religion relinquishing to science the intellectual sphere and thus being confined to the emotional realm of human nature. It was Martineau's defence of religion against the claims of some scientists that caused Owen Chadwick to remark that there came a time after Darwin when even orthodox churchmen came to look upon Martineau as a champion of faith.

Martineau retired from Manchester College in 1885 and over the following eight years wrote several important books, including *The Seat of Authority in Religion* (1890), *Types of Ethical Theory* (1895) and *A Study of Religion* (1888). However some of his work was already appearing dated by the time it came out in print. This in part was due to the fact that he was writing up and publishing his four-year cycle of lectures.

His major contribution was not his many articles on science and religion, nor his ethical or theological writing but his devotional writing. His two volumes of sermons, *Endeavours After the Christian Life* (1840) and *Hours of Thought on Sacred Things* (1876-9) still convey many splendid insights into the human condition and contain ideas and imagery that will continue to speak to other generations as well as they did to his own. His prayers also have a lasting quality. He both edited and wrote large sections of *Common Prayer for Christian Worship* (1862); and here for the first time, it has been suggested, Nonconformity produced a liturgical editor of rare genius. His *Home Prayers* (1892) contain deep devotion and beautiful expressions of the Christian faith. These prayers have often been reprinted in other anthologies, sometimes without acknowledgment.

Martineau was too broadminded to belong to any school. He was eclectic in his nature and gathered ideas from any source that appealed to his own intellectual and emotional character. His philosophical theology was shaped more by his personality and the movements of the age than by specific adherence to one particular school of thought. He in himself was a record of nineteenth-century theology; born only three years after the death of Kant and living on into the twentieth century, he engaged or commented on almost every theological personality or move-ment of the age, as can be seen from his volumes of collected *Essays, Reviews and Addresses* (1890-91).

THE CATHOLIC CHURCH AND ITS DIVERSITY

Martineau's idea of a catholic Church begins with the observation that there are real differences in people's perceptions of the Christian faith, and that these differences actually enrich the faith. Martineau illustrated his essential thesis by pointing out that there were greater differences between the 'doctrine' of St Mark's Gospel and the 'mystic depth' of St John's Gospel than between Augustine and Pelagius. Martineau held that the early period was able to span its differences because it was inspired, while the later period was unable to do this because it was withered up by contentions.[15] This illustration assumes that the Gospel writers were in some sort of spiritual harmony with one another in spite of their differences; and Martineau's initial proposition of a catholic Church containing a variety of different views has much to commend it. This phenomenon he maintained was demonstrated in miniature in certain denominations such as the Methodists and the Society of Friends, who held a variety of opinions, but subordinated their theological differences to the needs of the Christian Church and Christian worship.[16]

Martineau's position was supported by his own experience. He acknowledged that he had received far more from those who were outside his own church than from those within it:

> I am conscious that my deepest obligations, as a learner from others, are in almost every department to writers not of my own creed ... In Biblical interpretation, I derive from Calvin and Whitby the help that fails me in Crell and Belsham. In Devotional literature and religious thought, I find nothing of ours that does not pale before Augustine, Tauler and Pascal. And in the Poetry of the Church it is the Latin or the German hymns, or the lines of Charles Wesley, or of Keble, that fasten on my memory and heart, and make all else seem poor and cold.[17]

His practice of drawing from a wide catholic background also influenced his habits of worship. His friend, Professor Knight, recalled how, after 1872, Martineau would worship at Little Portland Street Chapel on Sunday morning, but that was not enough for him, so in the afternoons he went to Westminster Abbey where sometimes he heard Dean Stanley preach.[18]

Not only should individuals acknowledge the diversity of backgrounds to which they are indebted, but churches also should be aware of the varied roots from which their tradition has developed. He indicated in his correspondence with MacDonald the danger of tracing the history of their churches solely to Unitarian sources, as by implication this would preclude the possibility of being in communion with non-Unitarians as well.[19]

CHRIST BRINGS TOGETHER THOSE HOLDING DIVERSE VIEWS

Martineau's belief that Christ would bring together those of differing outlooks is perhaps best summed up by a hymn of Charles Wesley's which Martineau included in both his later hymn books:

> Ye different sects, who all declare
> Lo! here is Christ, or Christ is there!
> Your claim alas! ye cannot prove;
> Ye want the genuine mark of love.

To Wesley, and to Martineau, the division of sects was not a matter of doctrine: it was a failure of love. And both writers would see the person and example of Jesus Christ as able to draw all men unto himself:

> Scattered, O Lord, thy servants lie,
> Till thou collect them with thine eye,
> Draw by the music of thy name,
> And charm into a beauteous frame.

> Join every soul that looks to thee
> In bonds of perfect charity;
> Greatest of gifts, thy love impart,
> And make us of one mind and heart.
> Charles Wesley, 1749[20]

Wesley and Martineau are not entirely at one on this point. The suggestion in Charles Wesley's hymn is that through the love of Christ believers would come to a common mind and a common understanding of the Christian faith. He expressed this in another well-known hymn: 'Even now we think and speak the same, And cordially agree; Concentred all, through

Jesu's name, In perfect harmony.'[21] Martineau's view differed in that he believed that through the love of Christ unity could be found as individuals came to appreciate and understand differing apprehensions of the Christian faith which contrasted with their own beliefs. In this Martineau was closer to John Wesley's ecclesiology than that of his brother Charles.

There was a pragmatic element also in Martineau's view of the Catholic Church. He held that to live out the faith was important, so that it became not a creed about God but an existence *in* God; if this was done the Christian would find himself alongside many unexpected friends. But beneath that pragmatic view lay the theological conviction (paralleled in F. D. Maurice's work): 'Sink deep into the inmost life of any Christian faith and you will touch the ground of all.'[22]

Notes

1. John Wesley, *44 Sermons*, ed. Edward H. Dudget, 2 vols (London: Epworth Press, 1921) II, pp. 139–40.
2. Ibid., p. 454.
3. *Letters of John James Tayler*, ed. J. H. Thom, 2 vols (London: Longman Green, 1872) II, p. 311.
4. James Martineau, *Essays, Reviews and Addresses* (London: Longman Green, 1890–91), II, p. 520.
5. *Letters of John James Tayler*, II, p. 324.
6. The aims of the Free Christian Union, as Martineau saw them, are set out in *Essays, Reviews and Addresses*, II, p. 509.
7. Arthur Sidgwick and Eleanor Sidgwick, *Henry Sidgwick: A Memoir* (London: Macmillan, 1906) p. 189.
8. *Letters of John James Tayler*, II, p. 324.
9. *The Inquirer*, 27 June 1868,Vol. XXVII, p. 407.
10. *Letters of John James Tayler*, II, p. 313.
11. *Letters of John James Tayler*, II, p. 324.
12. Arthur Sidgwick and Eleanor Sidgwick, *Henry Sidgwick: A Memoir*, p. 192.
13. John James Tayler, *The Catholic Church: The Want of Our Time*, pp. 5 and 6.
14. *The Catholic Church*, p. 45.
15. Martineau, *Essays, Reviews and Addresses*, II, p. 76.
16. James Martineau, *The Church of the Future* (Liverpool, 1871 (pamphlet)) p. 17.
17. Martineau, *Essays, Reviews and Addresses*, II, p. 375.

18. William Knight, *Retrospects* (London: Smith & Albert 1904), p. 105.
19. *The Inquirer*, 27 August 1859, pp. 763–4.
20. James Martineau, *Hymns for the Christian Church and Home* (17th edn, London, 1867), no. 241.
21. *The Methodist Hymn Book* (London: Epworth Press, 1933), no. 745.
22. James Martineau, *Studies of Christianity*, p.412. Maurice said, 'my business, because I am a theologian, and have no vocation except for theology, is not to build, but to dig, to show that economics and politics . . . must have a ground beneath themselves, that society is not be made anew by arrangements of ours, but is to be regenerated by finding the law and ground of its order and harmony, the only secret of its existence in God.' Alec Vidler, *The Theology of F. D. Maurice* (London: SCM Press, 1948, p. 12).

8

SPIRITUALITY IN THE ANGLICAN
TRADITION

GEOFFREY ROWELL

At the beginning of his book with the simple but daunting title,
Holiness, the late Donald Nicholl wrote wise words. 'One truly
holy person is worth more than any number of books about
holiness.'[1] He went on to remind his readers that knowledge of
holiness is not just another form of knowledge, such as the
knowledge we might have about mathematics, physics, or
geology.

> At the opposite pole from pure mathematics, knowledge of
> holiness is not concerned with abstract concepts which are
> totally unrelated to this concrete, material, living world in
> space and time and which do not affect our lives in any
> essential way. On the contrary it is concerned with concrete
> reality, with how persons assume total responsibility for the
> material living world in which they find themselves at a par-
> ticular place and a particular time. Moreover ... holiness
> ... turns the tables on us, so to speak ... You imagined that
> you had taken the initiative in pursuit of the Holy One, and
> then realise that in truth it was the Holy One who initiated
> the pursuit.[2]

To speak of holiness you have to be engaged in the pursuit of
holiness.

> Unless a person is ascending by degrees towards complete
> holiness, being changed at every step, that person cannot be
> said to be truly studying holiness. In fact one can affirm quite
> confidently that if a person claims to have studied holiness,
> but has not been changed in the course of doing so, then it
> was not holiness that he was studying but something else.[3]

The quest for holiness is the quest for God, and that quest turns
out to be God's search for us. In the end we have to hear and

participate in and even play the music, and not just analyse the structure of the symphony and detect the complex inter-weaving of themes and variations. As John Bowker emphasized at the end of his first series of Wilde Lectures, *The Sense of God*, quoting lines from Trollope's novel, *The Eustace Diamonds*,[4]

> 'Lucy, do give me that hunchy bit,' said Nina.
> ' "Hunchy" is not in the dictionary,' said Cecilia.
> 'I want it on my plate and not in the dictionary,' said Nina.

Christian spirituality implies an understanding of what it is to be human, and what it is to grow as a human being. It is about what an earlier age would have called 'experimental religion'. The Christian theologian starts with the conviction that human beings are made 'in the image of God', they are open to transcendence, and are related by their very existence to the source of all that is, the Alpha, the first cause, the ground of being, the One who let (and lets) all things be. That 'ground of being' is at least personal, for it must be at least adequate to a universe in which personal being emerges, for at the heart of human self-understanding is the overriding and compelling knowledge that we are persons, those born out of relatedness, and called to find our end in and through related-ness. The Christian theologian goes on to affirm that the source of all being has disclosed its being and character as love. What we speak of as 'revelation' is the disclosure in many and varied ways (but with particular points of concentration) of that being. The Creator is known as a communion of love, and to say that we are made in the image of God is to speak of our fundamental identity as being found within that commu-nion. Jesus said that there were two great commandments, inti-mately related to each other. The first was the love of God with all our heart and mind and soul and strength, and the second the love of neighbour as ourselves – commandments I once heard a Christian psychologist describe as 'the highest heuristic possibilities'!

Human nature made in the image of the Trinitarian God, who is its Alpha, is to find in that same God the Omega, the goal and measure of personal growth. We were created by grace – not by any compulsion on the part of God, but by his free choosing in love to allow the world in which we come to

be to exist. Theologians have spoken of the 'lure' or attractiveness of God, and that 'lure' or 'attractiveness' is modulated in
three compelling ways, the search for what is true, what is
indeed the case (a correspondence theory of truth, not simply
a coherence theory); the quest for what is the good, the source
of value; and the beauty which engages our attention, and
spills over into our being as we so attend, what Dante called
'that light which once a man has seen he can never turn away
from'. That truth, that goodness and that beauty are alike
personal in character – hence in the Scriptures the importance
of the theme of the 'face of God': Jacob wrestling with the
mysterious figure, with indeed God himself, and naming the
place Peniel, because he has seen God face to face (Gen.
32.30); the Psalmist crying out 'Seek ye my face ... thy face
Lord will I seek' (Ps. 27.8 AV); and the glory of God for Paul
seen in the 'face' of Jesus Christ, a face whose compelling
contemplation turns us into its likeness 'from one degree of
glory to another' (2 Cor. 3.18; 4.6). Irenaeus may have been
mistaken in his reading of Genesis in failing to recognize the
Hebrew parallelism between ἐικων and ὁμοιωσις, but his
instinct was sure in speaking of our being fashioned in the
image of God, and being drawn by grace to attain his likeness.
It is this sense of the dynamic of personhood in relation to God
(we can recall Meister Eckhart's dictum that 'grace is never a
stationary thing, it is always found in a becoming') that underlies the doctrine so central to the Greek Fathers of θεωσισ,
'deification'. This is best known in the epigram of Athanasius
('God became man that man might become God'),[5] but it is
Maximus the Confessor who points more precisely to our
human vocation, the lure that is in our being and in our heart
(remembering that the heart in Scripture is not the place of
feeling, but of choosing and willing). As Vladimir Lossky
summarizes Maximus' teaching: 'In deification we are by
grace ... all that God is by nature, save only identity of
nature. We remain creatures while becoming God by grace, as
Christ remained God in becoming man by the Incarnation.'[6]

We are to be 'changed into his likeness from glory to glory –
from one degree of glory to another'. Δοξα, a glory, with the
Hebrew *kabod* behind it, speaks of the very being and character
of God, a being and character which is a dazzling darkness, as

the tradition of apophatic theology reminds us, because the God in whose image we are made, as the person we are, is in the end 'mystery'. God recedes in the face of definitions, and definitions inevitably recede in the face of God. So, too, does the elusive 'I', the 'I' that is known only in relationship, and ultimately only fully in the perfect relationship of grace and love which is the love of the Trinitarian God. Even that fullness, that πλερωμα, the utter fullness of God, which St Paul speaks of our receiving, is something which can never be limited or circumscribed because of the very infinity of God. Like all relationships of love it is known, as Gregory of Nyssa expressed it, in an ἐπεκτασις, a thirsting for a union which is transfiguring and transforming, always a dynamic relationship and never a static perfection – 'More love! More love! More love' as the dying Dr Pusey, that most ecstatic of the Oxford Movement Fathers, exclaimed.[7]

'Our hearts' – the core of our willing, choosing, centred being – 'are restless until they rest in God,' said St Augustine in an often cited phrase. Luther in the same tradition spoke of the 'love of the heart making both God and idol'. Paul Tillich's language of 'ultimate concern' may be said to express this in another way. And Feuerbach, who resolved all into subjectivity – God as human aspiration projected and patterned on the heavens – may from one point of view be seen as a 'broken-down Augustinian'. So in this theological perspective the lure, the attractiveness of God, is discovered at the centre of our being. It is a love which motivates us as being human; and yet a love which needs to be 'set in order', for our human condition is fallen and flawed. The doctrine of total depravity, taught by some Protestant theological traditions, is and must be wrong if what is implied is that we are dark through and through, that the image of God is completely blotted out. But interpret it as meaning 'flawed in our totality' – there is no part of our human being which is not in some way or another flawed and distorted – our reason, our affections, our desires – and it makes much more sense. So when that Anglican poet T. S. Eliot spoke in the *Four Quartets* – a poem that it is as much about the spiritual journey as about creative writing – of 'the purification of the motive in the ground of our beseeching' (a phrase echoing Julian of Norwich), he was speaking out of that long tradition of how our hearts may find their rest in God, and how our distorted self-centred loving may be realigned by the magnet of God's self-giving love (the grace and κοινωνια, communion, belonging-togetherness of the Holy Spirit), a love made known to us in Jesus Christ. At the end of 'Little Gidding', the last of the *Quartets*, we find the words which sum up the Omega of our human pilgrimage.

> A condition of complete simplicity
> (Costing not less than everything)
> And all shall be well and
> All manner of thing shall be well
> When the tongues of flame are in-folded
> Into the crowned knot of fire
> And the fire and the rose are one.[8]

The 'condition of complete simplicity (Costing not less than everything)' – that 'purity of heart', which Kierkegaard said was 'to will one thing' – is a single-mindedness, not the compromising, shifting, deceitful double-mindedness of a life which is not drawn into the single attentiveness to God, which is the indwelling in the life of Jesus, who is the Way, the Truth and the Life.

And 'all shall be well', all shall share in that felicity or beatitude, the blessedness spoken of by Augustine and Dante, and no less in the English tradition by George Herbert, Henry Vaughan and Thomas Traherne, and many, many others. And what will that mean? It is a Trinitarian resolution. The 'tongues of flame', the transfiguring of each person as the tongues of the fire of the Spirit danced on the heads of the apostles at Pentecost – those unique, personal 'diagrams of God's glory' (as Charles Williams put it), those 'tongues of flames are in-folded Into the crowned knot of fire'. The Holy Spirit, whose gift and reality is κοινωνια, the love and the love-knot of the Trinity, is the gatherer into the 'communion' of saints. 'The Bible knows nothing of solitary religion' was advice Wesley took to heart, for unlike the Victorian lady who said on being invited to an evangelistic rally, 'But, O my dear, who would care to be saved in a crowd!', the Christian faith is a gathering into a common life, but a common life which values and does not expunge or repress the uniqueness of each person. The 'knot of fire' is 'crowned' because the life-giving, sanctifying Spirit is God (for the one who makes us partakers of the divine nature cannot be less than the self-giving love of God himself). That means that 'the fire and the rose are one', the fire of the Spirit, which is purifying, purging and the light of glory, and the rose, which in its pulsating, attractive beauty was for Dante the vision of God.

Such, at least in part, is the theology of the Christian journey, of that sanctification which is at the heart of the Christian life. That journey, the process of a growing into the likeness of God, is what Eliot speaks of as demanding 'a life-time's death in love'.[9] So in the tradition of the Church ascetic and mystical theology have always gone hand in hand: the former relating to the discipline and training, the latter attempting to express the reality of the working of the Spirit in Christian life, the nature of the transfiguring union with God which is at the heart of prayer.

In the first part of this paper I have tried to set out the understanding of the theology of Christian praying and living, the theology of becoming holy, that is at the heart of what we call Christian spirituality. We must now look more specifically at the Anglican tradition, though everything I have said so far I have said as an Anglican bishop out of the Anglican tradition. Let us now look at some of the characteristics of that tradition.

First let me remind you of just a few of the vast range of writers who have as Anglicans sought to reflect on this Christian way of holiness. The inheritance is rich indeed, and these names (and books) are only a fragment of what might be mentioned. So, in roughly chronological order, John Jewel (*Apology for the Church of England*); Richard Hooker (*The Laws of Ecclesiastical Polity*); Edmund Spenser, the poet; Bishop Lancelot Andrewes; George Herbert, priest and poet; Bishop John Cosin; Herbert Thorndike; Mark Frank; Bishop Jeremy Taylor (*Holy Living* and *Holy Dying*); Thomas Traherne (*Centuries of Meditation*); Archbishop Robert Leighton; the Cambridge Platonists; Bishop Thomas Ken, whose *Manual of Prayers* for Winchester Scholars includes his famous morning and evening hymns; Henry Scougal and the Aberdeen doctors; William Law (*A Serious Call to a Devout and Holy Life*; *Christian Perfection*; *The Way of Love*); John and Charles Wesley (their hymns, and John's (controversial) teaching on Christian perfection); Joseph Butler (*Sermons at the Rolls Chapel*); John Kettlewell (*The Practical Believer*; *The Measures of Christian Obedience*); William Wilberforce (*A Practical View*); Hannah More (*Practical Piety*); Henry Venn; Samuel Taylor Coleridge (*Aids to Reflection*); John Keble; John Henry Newman; Edward Pusey; Frederick Denison Maurice; Richard Benson; Henry Scott Holland; Bishop Edward King; Studdert Kennedy; Evelyn Underhill; Archbishop William Temple; T. S. Eliot; Archbishop Michael Ramsey; Austin Farrer. And that is but scratching the surface.

Second, we have to remember that the Church of England did not start at the Reformation. 'Ecclesia Anglicana' reaches back even beyond the mission of Augustine in 597. There was an earlier British Christianity, and some of that 'Celtic' inheritance is now being reclaimed, though with a certain amount of projection and interpretation. At the Reformation, as Eamonn Duffy and others have made clear, much that was at the centre of popular religion was swept away, but on the other hand we must not underestimate the impact of an English Bible, and services in the English tongue. Having some experience of the Church of Ethiopia where lengthy services are still chanted in Ge'ez, the ancient sacral language, one can see the impact of aural understanding when texts moved from Latin to English. Scripture was the fundamental text, and Scripture therefore, both for theological reasons and for the reasons of availability through printing, and because it was something newly heard, became of prime significance.

Third, there was the seeking of common prayer. Printing is inextricably bound up with this both as possibility and in reality. Printing creates uniformity, just as the information technology explosion of our own day presses towards diversity. A printed book could be imposed, and local divergence and diversity could be ironed out. The Book of Common Prayer is the foundation of Anglicanism as we know it. And what are the characteristics of that spirituality?

1. It is Benedictine in character. There is an importance given to the Daily Office, to Morning and Evening Prayer – a simple rhythm that moved out of the monastery and into the parish. It is an office which is grounded in reading Scripture, and in the recitation of psalms and the scriptural canticles.

Mattins and Evensong are, like almost all the Prayer Book services, in one sense little more than Scripture turned to prayer – versicles and responses, the ancient collects, are either quotations from Scripture or prayers built on Scripture.

2. The Holy Communion is at the centre, and the celebration of the Eucharist is intended to be for the purpose of communion. At the heart of it is the 'receiving of communion', and that phrase is one we would do well to ponder. What we receive is κοινωνια, 'belonging togetherness', but a 'belonging togetherness' which has at its heart the indwelling of Christ. As Cranmer's great Prayer of Humble Access puts it, the whole purpose is that by the mercy of God, 'We may evermore dwell in Him (Christ) and He in us'. As Cranmer himself put it in an early writing, the point of the Eucharist was not, as seemed so frequently to be the case in a non-communicating Latin Mass, that the congregation came to gaze on an external miracle, but that 'He be transubstantiate in us'. Indeed part of that sense may lie behind Cranmer's fractured traditional canon, where communion follows the Words of Institution, and only then do the communicants, united with Christ and bearing his life within them, offer and present themselves, their souls and bodies, to be 'a reasonable, holy and lively sacrifice unto Thee, humbly beseeching Thee that all we, who are partakers of this holy communion, may be fulfilled with Thy grace and heavenly benediction'.

3. The mysteries of the faith are celebrated and expressed in the Christian Year with its great festivals and commemoration of the grace of God in the lives of the saints, those whom John Keble called in a powerful phrase, 'the Saviour in His people crowned'.

4. And finally baptism, marriage, and burial draw into the Christian mystery three important stages in human life.

The General Thanksgiving in the 1662 Prayer Book, composed by Bishop Edward Reynolds of Norwich in 1661, gives thanks for 'our creation, preservation, and all the blessings of this life, but above all for thine inestimable love in the redemption of the world by our Lord Jesus Christ, for the means of grace and for the hope of glory'. Here is a very characteristic Anglican holding together, of creation, God's sustaining providence, and all the ordinary blessings of life, with redemption in

Christ on the one hand, and for the way that redemption is appropriated on the other – 'the means of grace' (prayer and the sacraments) – and that to which they all point, 'the hope of glory'. Creation – incarnation – cross and resurrection – and the life of the Spirit in the Church are all held together in one great prayer. The same holistic view is found in the great sermons of Bishop Lancelot Andrewes (1555–1626). Dr Nicholas Lossky's fine study, *Lancelot Andrewes, the Preacher* is subtitled *The Origins of the Mystical Theology of the Church of England*.[10] In it he elucidates how Andrewes' sermons on the great festivals of the Christian Year are profound explorations of the mystery of God's love and grace in redemption. Christmas, the festival of the incarnation, is the festival of Emmanuel, 'God-with-us', and that beginning of redemption and grace moves through the Passion ('Passion is but compassion at rebound; the cross is the very book of charity laid open before us') to the resurrection. The Ascension is given its full place, where 'the taking up of manhood into God' is brought to its culmination. (And it is worth noting here how significant has been the place accorded to the doctrine of the high priesthood of Christ in the Anglican tradition – signified, amongst other things, by the number of commentaries on Hebrews written by Anglicans in the nineteenth century, as well as in the hymns of Bishop Christopher Wordsworth and William Bright in the same period.) And beyond the Ascension there is the feast of Pentecost, the feast of 'Christ in us' which complements and fulfils the descent of incarnation. Lossky notes how, in both the liturgical sermons, and in the 'Preces Privatae', Andrewes' spirituality is shaped by the rhythm of prayer and celebration of the Prayer Book and the Christian year. He comments:

His prayer, which tends to become for him a perpetual prayer ... reveals an acute sense of the sanctification of every moment of time, without however being driven into a kind of atemporal ecstasy. The time of history subsists. But it is not the only time that is real. The time of salvation – the liturgical year – is just as real, if not more so. And the two times interpenetrate one another in the constant relationship of man to God.[11]

Lossky goes on to affirm that for Lancelot Andrewes spirituality (a modern term Andrewes does not use) is intimately linked to theology, for 'spirituality' is 'the ecclesial experience, in the Church, of the union of man with God, and not an individualistic pietism'.

> Theology ... far from being a speculative intellectual system to do with God, is a translation in terms that can be transmitted of this same ecclesial experience. It is consequently a vision of God and not a system of thought. Theology without spirituality would then be a sterile science; spirituality without theology, that is, without being rooted in right doctrine, would be enthusiasm to the point of hysteria ... Andrewes puts all his learning at the service of attaining to the end: to convert his hearers to the experience of God in the rectitude of the *Lex credendi*, which cannot but be in profound harmony with the *lex orandi*.[12]

The final point that should be made – for it is characteristic of Anglican spirituality, and not only, though most powerfully, of Andrewes – is the 'patristic' roots of that theology and devotion. In particular the Greek Fathers are drawn upon, who are profoundly Trinitarian, teach the doctrine of θεωσισ, and hold together creation and incarnation with a clear sense that sacraments in particular are framed within an understanding of the world as sacramental.

It is moreover a further characteristic of the Anglican tradition of spirituality that creation and incarnation belong together. You find it in Thomas Traherne's *Centuries of Meditation*, and particularly in the wonderful passage in which he speaks of the vision of the Hereford of his childhood as a kind of foretaste in microcosm of the City of God. You find it too in John Keble's poem from 'The Christian Year' for Septuagesima Sunday, the Sunday with creation readings. It was taken into Anglican hymn books, though is not now much sung.

> There is a book who runs may read,
>   Which heavenly truth imparts;
> And all the lore its scholars need,
>   Pure eyes and heavenly hearts.

> . . .

The moon above, the Church below,
  A wondrous race they run,
But all their radiance, all their glow,
  Each borrows of its sun.

The dew of heaven is like thy grace
  It steals in silence down,
Yet where it lights the favoured place
  By richest fruits is known.

. . .

Two worlds are ours: 'tis only sin
  Forbids us to descry
The mystic heaven and earth within,
  Plain as the sea and sky.

Thou who hast given me eyes to see
  And love this sight so fair,
Give me a heart to find out Thee,
  And read Thee everywhere.[13]

The glory of God shines in creation. The images are drawn from the Psalms, and from the simplest things of the natural order (dew and grace, refreshing and unobserved). The world is an index of the presence of God, a sacramental setting for human life.

Following on from this theme of creation is the strong sense in many Anglican theologians of the incarnation as the fulfilment of God's purposes in creation, rather than occasioned as a rescue operation after the fall of Adam. According to this line of theological thinking it was always God's purpose to join himself so closely to his creation that he knew it from the inside. There was a κενωσισ in creation, in God bringing into being that which was other than God, and there was a similar κενωσισ in incarnation. There are more than strong echoes of this doctrine in the Greek Fathers, but in the medieval West this view of the incarnation became one particularly associated with Duns Scotus. I suspect Anglicans picked it up from the Greek Fathers, but it is notable how it is found in the Anglican Newman, in F. D. Maurice, in Bishop Westcott (who gives a superb exposition of it in the appendix entitled 'The Doctrine of Creation' in his commentary on the Johannine Epistles),[14] in William Temple, and in Charles Williams.

Keble's exposition of the sacramental character of creation was embodied in a poem. One of the striking things about the Anglican tradition is the central place poetry plays within it. 'Poetry', wrote Samuel Taylor Coleridge, 'has a logic of its own, as severe as that of science; and more difficult because more subtle and dependent on more, and more and fugitive causes'.[15] The seventeenth century gives us George Herbert, Henry Vaughan, John Donne, and Thomas Traherne. ('It is the glory of His high estate, and that which I for evermore admire, He is an act that doth communicate.')[16] The eighteenth century gives us the Wesleys.

> Heavenly Adam, Life divine
> Change my nature into thine!
> Move and spread throughout my soul,
> Actuate and fill the whole.
> Be it I no longer now
> Living in the flesh, but thou.
>
> Changed from glory into glory,
> Till in heaven we take our place,
> Till we cast our crowns before Thee,
> Lost in wonder, love and praise.[17]

The nineteenth century gives us not only Wordsworth and Coleridge, but John Keble, Newman (though admittedly a better writer of prose than poetry), Christina Rossetti, and many great writers and translators of hymns. Again we should note how shaping are good theological hymns (and how debilitating are so many of the ditties that today are often substituted for them in the name of modernization or renewal). With this I would want to link the whole Anglican choral tradition, for how can one speak of the mystery of God without acknowledging the power of music to evoke and to praise that mystery? It was Professor Stephen Prickett who pointed out in his book, *Romanticism and Religion*, how powerful were the literary premises from which Anglicans started at that period in expressing their theology, and how these had passed with Newman and others into the Church of Rome.[18] And it was John Coulson who pointed out in relation first to Newman

(*Newman and the Common Tradition*) and then more generally (*Religion and Imagination*) the 'fiduciary character' of theological language.[19]

Anglicans have never been very good at systematic theology as either the scholastics or Protestant orthodoxy understood it. The close relationship between theology and devotion, '*lex orandi, lex credendi*', is in one way a safeguarding of the mystery of God. When Newman wrote, in his tract on rationalism in religion, that 'to say that Christianity is a revelation is not to deny that it is also a mystery', he went on to say that it is light and darkness at the same time. It is like the dim outline of mountains seen at twilight ... Creeds are but the 'symbol' of faith, profoundly true, yet never encompassing the mystery of the God to which they are intended to point.[20] The Tractarians saw the poet as resembling the prophet, someone of deep insight, penetrating in power, a doctrine lying hid in language. The liturgy and rhythm of the Book of Common Prayer has engraved this sense deep on the Anglican (and English) consciousness, and kept Anglican theology close to its prayed roots.

If poetry has been powerful, then liturgy as something enacted has been also shaping, though more at some periods than others. Anglicans have battled over the external symbols of worship, and at its best that worship has been a real door to the sacred. When Fr Mackonochie, the ritualist priest who was the first vicar of St Alban's, Holborn, was asked to justify his ritual practices, he replied in a powerful phrase, that it was 'the barest alphabet of reverence for so divine a mystery'. Again we come back to the mystery of grace, the mystery of our being, which worship opens up to the mystery of God. Christian spirituality made up of the disciplines of prayer, worship and Christian living is that pattern by which, in the different traditions of Christendom, we are enabled to grow into God, and live the life of the coming kingdom. It is the working out of 'Thy kingdom come, Thy will be done, On earth as it is in heaven'.

There are many Anglican writers who could exemplify this, but Thomas Traherne, with his sense of the glory of God in creation and the glory to which men and women are called and enabled by grace, can stand for them all as a conclusion.

The things we treat of are great and mighty. They touch the essence of every soul, and are of infinite concernment, because the felicity that is eternal is acquired by them. I do not mean immortal only, but worthy to be eternal; and it is impossible to be happy without them. We treat of man's great and sovereign end, of the nature of blessedness, and of the means to attain it ... My design is to reconcile men to God, and make them fit to delight in Him; and that my last end is to celebrate His praises, in communion with the angels. Wherein I beg the concurrence of the reader, for we can never praise Him enough, nor be fit to praise Him. No other man, at least, can make us so, without our own willingness and endeavour to do it.

Above all, pray to be sensible of the excellency of the Creation, for upon the due sense of its excellency the life of felicity wholly dependeth. Pray to be sensible of the excellency of divine laws, and of all goodness which your soul comprehendeth. Covet a lively sense of all you know of the excellency of God and of Eternal Love, of your own excellency, and of the worth and value of all objects whatsoever. For to feel is as necessary as to see their glory.[21]

Notes

1. Donald Nicholl, *Holiness* (London: Darton, Longman & Todd, 1981), p. 5.
2. Ibid., pp. 9–10.
3. Ibid., p. 11.
4. Anthony Trollope, *The Eustace Diamonds* (1873) (Oxford, 1968), p. 134. Quoted in J. Bowker, *The Sense of God: Sociological, Anthropological and Psychological Approaches to the Origin of the Sense of God* (Oxford: Clarendon Press, 1973), p. 180.
5. Athanasius, *On the Incarnation of the Word*, 54.3.
6. Vladimir Lossky, *The Mystical Theology of the Eastern Church* (Cambridge: James Clarke, 1957), p. 87.
7. Jean Daniélou in the introduction to his selection of texts from Gregory of Nyssa's mystical writings identifies this doctrine as Gregory's major contribution to the theology of the spiritual life. As Malherbe and Ferguson put it: 'There is no stopping place in the racecourse of virtue.' J. Daniélou and H. Musurillo, *From Glory to Glory: Texts from Gregory of Nyssa's Mystical Writings*

(New York: Scribner, 1962), pp. 46ff.; A. J. Malherbe and E. Ferguson, 'Introduction', *Gregory of Nyssa: The Life of Moses* (Classics of Western Spirituality; New York: Paulist Press, 1978), pp. 12–13.

8. T. S. Eliot, 'Little Gidding' V, *Collected Poems 1909–1962* (London: Faber & Faber, 1963), pp. 222–3.

9. T. S. Eliot, 'Dry Salvages' V, *Collected Poems*, p. 212.

10. Nicholas Lossky, *Lancelot Andrewes, the Preacher (1555–1626): The Origins of the Mystical Theology of the Church of England*, tr. A. Louth (Oxford: Clarendon Press, 1991).

11. Ibid., p. 29.

12. Ibid., p. 31.

13. John Keble, *The Christian Year* (1827), Poem for Septuagesima Sunday.

14. B. F. Westcott, *The Epistles of St John* (London, 1883), pp. 273–315.

15. S. T. Coleridge, *Biographia Literaria*, ed. J. Shawcross (Oxford: Clarendon Press, 1907), I, p. 4.

16. 'The Anticipation' in G. I. Wade and A. E. Dobell (eds) *The Poetical Works of Thomas Traherne* (London: P. J. & A. E. Dobell, 1932).

17. Stanza from 'Since the Son has set you free', *Methodist Hymn Book*, 568; stanza from 'Love Divine all loves excelling', *Methodist Hymn Book*, 431. Quoted by H. A. Hodges and A. M. Allchin, *A Rapture of Praise: Hymns of John and Charles Wesley* (London: Hodder & Stoughton, 1966), pp. 121, 120.

18. Stephen Prickett, *Romanticism and Religion: The Tradition of Coleridge and Wordsworth in the Victorian Church* (Cambridge: Cambridge University Press, 1976).

19. John Coulson, *Newman and the Common Tradition: A Study in the Language of Church and Society* (Oxford: Clarendon Press, 1970); *Religion and Imagination: 'In Aid of a Grammar of Assent'* (Oxford: Clarendon Press, 1981).

20. J. H. Newman, 'On the Introduction of Rationalistic Principles into Revealed Religion', *Essays Critical and Historical* (London: Pickering, 1872), I, pp. 41–2.

21. Margaret Bottrall (ed.), *The Way to Blessedness: Thomas Traherne's 'Christian Ethicks'* (London: Faith Press, 1962), pp. 18, 20.

FURTHER READING

General Reading

DICTIONARIES

There are many good articles to be found in dictionaries. Especially
useful are:

Bouyer, Louis, Leclercq, Jean and Vandenbroucke, François (eds),
A History of Christian Spirituality, vols 1 and 2 (London: Burns
Oates and Seabury, 1982).

Cabrol, Fernand and Leclercq, Henri (eds), *Dictionnaire d'archéologie
chrétienne et de liturgie*, 15 vols (Paris: Letouzy et Ané, 1907–53).

McGinn, Bernard, Meyendorff, John and Leclercq, Jean (eds), *A
History of Christian Spirituality*, vols 1, 2, 3 (New York: Crossroads,
1985ff.).

Wakefield, Gordon (ed.), *Dictionary of Christian Spirituality* (London:
SCM Press, 1982).

All these contain extensive bibliographies. For up-to-date bibliographies, see:

Cross, F. L., and Livingstone, E. A. (eds), *The Oxford Dictionary of the
Christian Church* (Oxford: Oxford University Press, 1997).

Jones, Cheslyn, Wainwright, Gordon and Yarnold, Edward (eds),
The Study of Spirituality (London: SPCK, 1980).

Many volumes of translations of classic texts of Western spirituality
can be found in the volumes of Penguin Classics and also in
McGinn, Bernard (ed.), *Classics of Western Spirituality* (New York:
Paulist Press, 1970ff.).

GENERAL BACKGROUND BOOKS

Older studies in the area of Christian ascetic theology are often
illuminating for the relation of spirituality to theology on a wide
scope:

Balthasar, Hans Urs von, *On Prayer – The Glory of the Lord: Theological
Aesthetics*, tr. A. V. Littledale (London: SPCK, 1973).

Bloom, Anthony, *The Essence of Prayer* (London: Darton, Longman
& Todd, 1986).

Butler, C., *Western Mysticism* (London: Constable, 1922).

Inge, W. R., *Christian Mysticism* (London: Methuen, 1899).
Kirk, K. E., *The Vision of God* (London: Longman, Green and Co., 1931).
Knowles, D., *What is Mysticism?* (London: Burns & Oates, 1967).
Underhill, Evelyn, *Mysticism* (London: Methuen, 1911).

RECENT BOOKS

More recent studies are usually of more precise areas:

Merton, Thomas, *Contemplative Prayer* (New York: Herder, 1969).
Merton, Thomas, *Seeds of Contemplation* (New York: New Directions, 1948).
Mursell, G., *Out of the Deep: Prayer as Protest* (London: Darton, Longman & Todd, 1989).
Tugwell, Simon, *Ways of Imperfection* (London: Darton, Longman & Todd, 1984).
Ward, Benedicta, *Prayers and Meditations of St Anselm with the Proslogion* (Harmondsworth: Penguin Books, 1979).
Williams, Rowan, *The Wound of Knowledge* (London: Darton, Longman & Todd, 1979).

Books by Chapter

2 PRAYER IN EVAGRIUS OF PONTUS AND THE MACARIAN HOMILIES

Sources

Evagrius, *On Prayer*, PG 79: 1165–1200; tr. G. E. H. Palmer, Philip Sherrard and Kallistos Ware, *The Philokalia*, vol. I (London and Boston: Faber & Faber, 1979), pp. 55–71.
Evagrius, *Praktikos*, ed. Antoine and Claire Guillaumont, *Sources chrétiennes* 170–171 (Paris: Cerf, 1971); tr. John Eudes Bamberger (Cistercian Studies 4; Spencer: Cistercian Publications, 1970).
Evagrius, *Gnostikos*, ed. Antoine and Claire Guillaumont, *Sources chrétiennes* 356 (Paris: Cerf, 1989).
Evagrius, *Gnostic Chapters*, ed. Antoine Guillaumont, *Patrologia Orientalis* XXVIII, 1 (134) (Paris: Firmin-Didot, 1958).
Muyldermans, J. *Evagriana, Le Muséon*, 44 (1931).
Muyldermans, J. *Evagriana Syriaca* (Bibliothèque du Muséon 31; Louvain: Publications Universitaires, 1952).
Diadochus of Photice, *On Spiritual Knowledge and Discernment: One Hundred Texts*, ed. Edouard des Places, *Sources chrétiennes* 5 bis

(Paris: Cerf, 1959); tr. Palmer, Sherrard and Ware, *The Philokalia*, vol. I, pp. 252–96.

Gregory of Nyssa, *The Life of Moses*, ed. Jean Daniélou, *Sources chré-tiennes* 1 bis (Paris: Cerf, 1955); tr. Abraham J. Malherbe and Everett Ferguson (The Classics of Western Spirituality; New York: Paulist Press, 1978).

Isaac of Nineveh, *Mystic Treatises*, tr. A. J. Wensinck (Amsterdam: Koninklijke Akademie van Wetenschappen, 1923).

Issac of Nineveh, *The Ascetical Homilies*, tr. Dana Miller (Boston: Holy Transfiguration Monastery, 1984).

The Macarian Homilies, Collection I, ed. Heinz Berthold, 2 vols. *Die Griechischen Christlicher Schriftsteller der Ersten Jahrhunderte* (Berlin: Akademie-Verlag, 1973).

The Macarian Homilies, Collection II, ed. Hemann Dörries, Erich Klostermann and Matthias Kroeger, *Patristische Texte und Studien* 4 (Berlin: Gruyter, 1964); tr. George Maloney (The Classics of Western Spirituality (CWS; New York/Mahwah: Paulist Press, 1992).

Modern Works

Louth, Andrew, *The Origins of the Christian Mystical Tradition: From Plato to Denys* (Oxford: Clarendon Press, 1981).

Stewart, Columba, '*Working the Earth of the Heart': The Messalian Controversy in History, Texts, and Language to AD 431* (Oxford: Clarendon Press, 1991).

Stewart, Columba, *Cassian the Monk* (New York: Oxford University Press, 1998).

Tugwell, Simon, *Ways of Imperfection: An Exploration of Christian Spirituality* (London: Darton, Longman & Todd, 1984).

Ware, Kallistos, *The Orthodox Way* (rev. edn, New York: St Vladimir's Seminary Press, 1996).

3 FRIENDSHIP

Aelred of Rievaulx, *Spiritual Friendship*, tr. Mark Williams (London: University of Scranton Press, 1994).

Badhwar, N. K., *Friendship: A Philosophical Reader* (Ithaca, NY: Cornell University Press, 1993).

Cicero, *On the Good Life*, tr. Michael Grant (Harmondsworth: Penguin, 1971).

Derrida, Jacques, *Politics of Friendship*, tr. George Collins (London: Verso, 1997).

Fisk, Adele, *Friends and Friendship in the Monastic Tradition* (Cuernavaca: Centro Intercultural de Documentacion, 1970).
Letters of Anselm of Canterbury, tr. Walter Frolich (Kalamazoo: Cistercian Publications, 1990).
Lewis, C. S., *The Four Loves* (London: Geoffrey Bles, 1960).
McGuire, Brian, *Friendship and Community: The Monastic Experience, 350–1250* (Kalamazoo: Cistercian Publications, 1988).
McNamara, M. A., *Friendship in St. Augustine* (Fribourg: Fribourg University Press, 1958).
White, Caroline, *Christian Friendship in the Fourth Century* (Cambridge: Cambridge University Press, 1992).

4 THE ENGLISH MYSTICS

General

Glasscoe, Marion, *English Medieval Mystics: Games of Faith* (London: Addison Wesley Longman, 1993).
Knowles, D., *The English Mystical Tradition* (London: Burns & Oates, 1951).
Riehle, R. W., *The Middle English Mystics* (Salzburg, 1982).

Richard Rolle

Horstman, C., *Writings Ascribed to Richard Rolle and his Followers* (London, 1893).
Rolle, Richard, *The Fire of Love*, tr. Clifton Wolters (Harmondsworth: Penguin Books, 1972).
Hodgson, Phyllis, *Some Minor Works of Richard Rolle of Hampole* (London: John M. Watkins, 1923).
English Writings of Richard Rolle, tr. R. Allen (New York: Paulist Press, 1995).
Compar, F. M. M., *The Life and Lyrics of Richard Rolle* (London: Dent, 1928).

The Cloud

The Cloud of Unknowing and Related Treatises on Contemplative Prayer, ME text, ed. Phyllis Hodgson (Analecta Carthusiana; Salzburg: Institut für Anglistik und Amerikanistik, Universität Salzburg, 1982).
The Cloud of Unknowing, tr. Clifton Wolters (Harmondsworth: Penguin Books, 1961).
A Study of Wisdom, tr. Clifton Wolters (Oxford: S.L.G. Press, 1980).

The Cloud of Unknowing, tr. James Walsh (New York: Paulist Press, 1982).

John Clark, *Notes to the Cloud and the Book* (Salzburg: Institut für Anglistik und Amerikanistik, Universität Salzburg, 1996).

Walter Hilton

Hilton, W., *The Scale of Perfection*, tr. E. Underhill (London: Methuen, 1923).

Hilton, W., *The Scale of Perfection*, tr. J. Clark and R. Dorward (New York: Paulist Press, 1991).

Hilton, W., *Eight Chapters on Perfection and Angels' Song*, tr. R. Dorward (Oxford: S.L.G. Press, 1983).

Julian of Norwich

A Book of the Showings to the Anchoress Julian of Norwich, ME text, ed. E. Colledge and J. Walsh (CWS; Toronto: P.I.M.S., 1978). This Middle English text has been much criticized and though less complete the edition of one MS by M. Glasscoe may be preferred.

Julian of Norwich: A Revelation of Love, ME text, ed. M. Glasscoe (Exeter: University of Exeter, 1976).

Julian of Norwich: Showings, tr. E. Colledge and J. Walsh (New York: Paulist Press, 1978).

Margery Kempe

The Book of Margery Kempe, ME text, ed. S. B. Meech and H. E. Allen (London: published for the Early English Text Society by Oxford University Press, 1940).

The Book of Margery Kempe, tr. B. A. Windeatt (Harmondsworth: Penguin Books, 1985).

For an excellent recent discussion of Margery, see Santha Bhattacharji, *God is an Earthquake* (London: Darton, Longman & Todd, 1998).

5 THE SPANISH MYSTICS

Campbell, Roy, *Poems of St John of the Cross* (Spanish with verse translation) (London: Collins, 1960).

The Complete Works of St John of the Cross, tr. E. Allison Peers, 3 vols (London: Sheed & Ward, 1934/5).

The Complete Works of St Teresa, tr. E. Allison Peers, 3 vols (London: Sheed & Ward, 1946).

ᅟ

 FURTHER READING

Hamilton, Alastair, *Heresy and Mysticism in Sixteenth-Century Spain: The Alumbrados* (Cambridge: James Clarke, 1992).
O'Reilly, *From Ignatius Loyola to John of the Cross* (Aldershot: Variorum, 1995).
Peers, E. Allison, *Studies in the Spanish Mystics*, 3 vols (London: Sheldon Press, 1972).
Peers, E. Allison, *Spirit of Flame* (London: SCM Press, 1943).
Peers, E. Allison, *Mother of Carmel* (London: SCM Press, 1945).
Stein, E., *The Science of the Cross* (London: Burns & Oates, 1951).
Thompson, C., *The Poet and the Mystic* (Oxford: Oxford University Press, 1977).
Trueman Dicken, E. W., *The Crucible of Love* (London: Darton, Longman & Todd, 1963).
Williams, R. D., *Teresa of Avila* (London: Geoffrey Chapman, 1991).

6 WILLIAM LAW AND THE WESLEYS

Allchin, A. M., *The Rapture of Praise* (London: Hodder & Stoughton, 1966).
Brazier Green, J., *John Wesley and William Law* (London: Epworth Press, 1945).
Law, William, *A Serious Call and the Spirit of Love*, ed. G. Stanwood (New York: Paulist Press, 1978).
Lindstrom, H., *Wesley and Sanctification* (London: Epworth Press, 1956).
Rack, H. D., *Reasonable Enthusiast: John Wesley and the Rise of Methodism* (London: Epworth Press, 1989).
Stranks, C. J., *Anglican Devotion* (London: SCM Press, 1961).
Walker, A. K., *William Law, His Life and Work* (London: SPCK, 1973).
William Law, Selected Writings, ed. J. Louth (Manchester: Carcanet Press, 1990).
Whaling, F. (ed.), *John and Charles Wesley* (New York: Paulist Press; London: SPCK, 1981).

7 SPIRITUALITY AND UNITY

Carpenter, J. Estlin, *James Martineau* (London, 1905).
Rack, Henry D., *Reasonable Enthusiast, John Wesley and the Rise of Methodism* (London: Epworth Press, 1989).
Short, H. L., Bolam, C. G., Goring, J., Thomas, R., *The English Presbyterians* (London: Allen & Unwin, 1968).
Tayler, John James, *Letters*, ed. J. H. Thom, 2 vols (London, 1872).
Watson, J. R., *The English Hymn* (Oxford: Oxford University Press, 1977).

ᅟᅟ

ᅟ

8   SPIRITUALITY IN THE ANGLICAN TRADITION

Allchin, A. M., *The Dynamic of Tradition* (London: Darton, Longman & Todd, 1981).

Lossky, N., *Lancelot Andrewes the Preacher (1555-1626): The Origins of the Mystical Theology of the Church of England*, tr. A. Louth (Oxford: Clarendon Press, 1991).

More, P. E. and Cross, F. L. (eds), *Anglicanism* (London: SPCK, 1935).

Rowell, G., *The Vision Glorious* (Oxford: Clarendon Press, 1974).

Rowell, G. (ed.), *The English Religious Tradition and the Genius of Anglicanism* (Wantage: Ikon Publications, 1992).

Stranks, C. J., *Anglican Devotion* (London: SCM Press, 1981).

INDEX

activity 78, 82–3
Aelred of Rievaulx 33
Alonso de Madrid 69
alumbrados 71
Andrewes, Lancelot 132–3
Annesley, Samuel 101–2
Anselm 32, 42–3, 53, 62
apophatic prayer 15, 25
Aristotle 36–7
arrow prayers 24–6
ascetic life 8, 81
Augustine of Hippo 9, 32, 41–5, 70

Bacon, Francis 32
Baxter, Richard 101–2
Beckett, Samuel 33
Bernard of Clairvaux 10
Bernardino de Laredo 69
body, the, as place of Christ 7; in Evagrius 19–20, 22–3; in Macarian *Homilies* 22–3
Boehme, Jacob 97
Bowker, John 125

Cappadocian Fathers 5
Christ: as bridegroom 10; central to the Church 103–4; transfiguration 23
Church, defined by Christ's presence 103–7; unity 106–7, 120–1 *see also* Free Christian Union
Cicero 37
Clement of Alexandria 3
Cloud of Unknowing 54–7

contemplation 18–19
creation 134, 136–7

darkness 7, 11, 51, 56, 76–8, 83–7
David 35
Diadochus of Photice 25
Duns Scotus, John 48, 134

ecstasy 19, 23–4, 31
Eliot, T. S. 63, 127–8
Erasmus 70
erotic, idea of the 9–10, 87–8
Eucharist 7–8, 131
Evagrius of Pontus 14–27

face of God 6, 126
fellowship *see koinonia*
Francisco de Osuna 69
Free Christian Union 110–14
friendship 31–46

Gibbon, Edward 93–4
God: as 'Abba' 2; as mother 62, 86–7; presence in creation 134; seeing his face 6, 126
Gregory of Nyssa 5–7, 9, 10, 17
Gregory Palamas 20

Hausherr, Irénée 15
heart, the, in theology of Macarian *Homilies* 20–2
Hesychasts 20
Hilton, Walter 52–4
holiness 7–8, 98, 124
Holy Spirit 2, 11, 23, 128

Ignatius of Antioch 7
illuminati 71

The Society for Promoting Christian Knowledge (SPCK) was founded in 1698. It has as its purpose three main tasks:

- **Communicating the Christian faith in its rich diversity**
- **Helping people to understand the Christian faith and to develop their personal faith**
- **Equipping Christians for mission and ministry**

SPCK Worldwide serves the Church through Christian literature and communication projects in over 100 countries. Special schemes also provide books for those training for ministry in many parts of the developing world. SPCK Worldwide's ministry involves Churches of many traditions. This worldwide service depends upon the generosity of others and all gifts are spent wholly on ministry programmes, without deductions.

SPCK Bookshops support the life of the Christian community by making available a full range of Christian literature and other resources, and by providing support to bookstalls and book agents throughout the UK. SPCK Bookshops' mail order department meets the needs of overseas customers and those unable to have access to local bookshops.

SPCK Publishing produces Christian books and resources, covering a wide range of inspirational, pastoral, practical and academic subjects. Authors are drawn from many different Christian traditions, and publications aim to meet the needs of a wide variety of readers in the UK and throughout the world.

The Society does not necessarily endorse the individual views contained in its publications, but hopes they stimulate readers to think about and further develop their Christian faith.

For further information about the Society, please write to:
SPCK, Holy Trinity Church, Marylebone Road,
London NW1 4DU, United Kingdom.
Telephone: 0171 387 5282